PENGUIN  CLASSICS

ONE HUNDRED POETS, ONE POEM EACH

PETER MACMILLAN is a translator, poet and artist. His earlier version of the *One Hundred Poets, One Poem Each* (*Hyakunin isshu*) was awarded the Donald Keene Center Special Prize for the Translation of Japanese Literature and the Special Cultural Translation Prize from the Japan Society of Translators, both in 2008. He has also published a collection of poetry, *Admiring Fields*, while his series of prints, *Thirty-Six New Views of Mount Fuji*, has been widely exhibited in Japan and other countries. His translation of *The Tales of Ise* was published in Penguin Classics in 2016. Peter MacMillan is Translator in Residence at the National Institute of Japanese Literature.

T0200940

One Hundred Poets, One Poem Each

A Treasury of Classical Japanese Verse

Translated with a Commentary by
PETER MACMILLAN

PENGUIN BOOKS

PENGUIN CLASSICS

UK | USA | Canada | Ireland | Australia
India | New Zealand | South Africa

Penguin Books is part of the Penguin Random House group of companies
whose addresses can be found at global.penguinrandomhouse.com

A previous version of this translation was published in the USA by Columbia University Press 2008
Revised edition published in Penguin Classics 2018

013

Translation and Commentary copyright © Peter MacMillan, 2008, 2018

Set in 10.6/12.75 pt Sabon Next LT Pro
Typeset by Jouve (UK), Milton Keynes
Printed and bound in Great Britain by Clays Ltd, Elcograf S.p.A.

ISBN: 978-0-141-39593-7

www.greenpenguin.co.uk

Contents

ONE HUNDRED POETS,
ONE POEM EACH

List of Illustrations

The illustrations in the book have been taken from Yasushi Yokoiyama's complete series of the *Hyakunin isshu*'s one hundred poets. All images are courtesy of Peter MacMillan.

Introduction

What is the *One Hundred Poets*?

One Hundred Poets, One Poem Each (*Hyakunin isshu*) is a private compilation of poems dating to around 1230–40 and assembled by the renowned poet and scholar Fujiwara no Teika (1162–1241). The best-loved and most widely read of all Japanese poetry collections, it was also the first work of Japanese literature to be translated into English – by Frederick Victor Dickins (1838–1915) – in 1866. There are three main reasons for its popularity. Firstly, its compiler, Teika, a scholar, theoretician and philologist, was the most admired poet of his time. Secondly, as a collection of one hundred of the best poems by one hundred representative poets, it provides a convenient introduction to the finest Japanese poetry from the late seventh to the early thirteenth centuries. Finally, it has endured thanks in part to the countless paintings, illustrated editions, commentaries and even a card game that have been inspired by it.[1]

Along with *The Tales of Ise* and *The Tale of Genji*, the *One Hundred Poets* is one of the three most influential works of classical Japanese literature. It has had an almost inestimable influence on Japanese culture and the visual arts at every level: every major Japanese print (ukiyo-e) artist has illustrated the entire collection, for instance. For hundreds of years it was *the* primer of Japanese classical poetry, and even today it is still the most widely known collection of Japanese verse, despite the fact that most Japanese have only the vaguest idea of what the poems mean. There is no equivalent to this short collection in English literature; Shakespeare's sonnets may appear close, but less than half a dozen of them are widely taught in schools today, whereas in Japan this book is an essential part of every secondary-school curriculum.

Who was Fujiwara no Teika?

Fujiwara no Teika (also known as Sadaie) was born into a minor branch of the noble Fujiwara family in 1162. His father, Shunzei (poem 83 in this collection), was a poet and critic and, in that capacity, held the highest position at the Imperial Bureau of Poetry, unrivalled in his generation. In person, Teika is said to have been irascible and strikingly ugly; but he was recognized as a great poet and authority on *waka* poetry, and his reputation exceeded even his father's. Teika's poetic and editorial achievements include poetry collections (both official and private), several one-hundred-poem sequences, commentaries on older works and treatises on poetry. He was also known for his work in philology, including the conservation of many important writings of the Heian period (794–1185), such as *The Tale of Genji* and *The Tales of Ise*. His *Maigetsushō* (Monthly Notes; 1219) was his *Ars Poetica*, in which he established the canons of poetic taste that would remain influential in Japan for hundreds of years. In addition, he wrote numerous other poetic treatises, including the *Kindai shūka* (Superior Poems of Our Time; 1209) and *Eiga no taigai* (Outline of Composition; *c.*1222), while his own collection of poetry, the *Shūigusō* (The Dull Musings of a Chamberlain; 1216) contained over 3,500 poems. The *One Hundred Poets* is but one of many anthologies Teika compiled during his lifetime. Some of these were intended to be used as textbooks on poetry by aristocratic pupils, and they were still in use for hundreds of years after Teika's death. Though *One Hundred Poets* was not included among these, it became the textbook par excellence for aspiring poets for the next six hundred years.

Teika's reputation was established quite early. In 1192, he was one of the twelve poets who provided poems for the famous *Roppyakuban uta-awase* (Poetry Contest in Six Hundred Rounds), an important competition held at the house of the regent Fujiwara no Ryokei (see poem 91) and presided over by Shunzei.

Teika was initially excluded from the list of contributors of a poetry event held eight years later, in 1200, in which twenty-two poets were ordered by Emperor Gotoba (r. 1184–98) each to compose a one-hundred-poem sequence (known as *hyakushu* in Japanese). Teika was only included later thanks to his father's intercession, but Emperor Gotoba was extremely pleased with his selection of poems and as a result granted him access to the imperial palace, a much-coveted honour. A year later, Gotoba ordered thirty of the best poets (including himself and Teika) each to present a one-hundred-poem sequence as the basis for another poetry contest. And from 1201 Teika was also involved in the compilation of the *Shin-kokin wakashū* (New Collection of Poems Ancient and Modern), usually abbreviated to *Shin-kokinshū*, the eighth of the imperial *waka* anthologies that had been ordered since the *Kokin wakashū* (Collection of *Waka* Ancient and Modern), or *Kokinshū*, was commissioned in 905. Being asked to edit one of these collections amounted to being acknowledged as the foremost literary figure of the day.

Teika's troubled literary relationship with Emperor Gotoba dates from this period. A poet himself (see poem 99), and a key figure in the literary world of the time, Gotoba wished to be involved in the editing of the *Shin-kokinshū*. He and Teika disagreed over the final selection of poems, however, and not even the fact that forty-six of Gotoba's own poems were selected for inclusion seems to have assuaged the emperor's bitterness. Although Teika's relationship with Gotoba never recovered after this, he was none the less able to retain power and influence because of his connection with other government figures whose power was growing at that time. He was also close to Fujiwara no Kintsune (poem 96), the most influential politician of the period following the fall of Gotoba in 1198.

In 1232, Teika was appointed to compile the *Shin-chokusen wakashū* (New Imperial *Waka* Collection), or *Shin-chokusenshū*, making him the only poet up until then to have the honour of editing two imperial anthologies. (His son Tameie was later accorded the same honour.) It was completed in 1235 and it was during this decade, the 1230s, that he assembled the *One Hundred Poets*.

Many of Teika's early poems are intricate and difficult to understand, leading some to accuse him of composing 'faddish, groundless Zen-nonsense poems' (*shingi hikyo daruma-uta*).[2] The poems by Teika's father, Shunzei, were more contemplative in tone. He championed the literary ideal of *yūgen* and established it as one of the major styles of the age. The term is difficult to define, and its meaning has changed over time, but it favours an indirect, enigmatic form of expression. One of the finest examples of *yūgen*, according to Shunzei, was a poem from the *Shin-kokinshū*, by Saigyo (see poem 86), who abandoned the world to become a monk:

> I have no heart, nor pathos,
> and yet I feel moved
> looking out over the marsh
> where snipe are rising
> in the autumn dusk.

> *(Kokoronaki / mi ni mo aware wa/ shirarekeri /*
> *shigi tatsu sawa no / aki no yugure)*

The type of poetry favoured by Teika and his younger contemporaries, by contrast, conformed to the *yōen* (lofty and ethereal) style, which combined dream-like imagery and allusions to earlier works to produce poems of remarkable subtlety. The following poem, composed for a poetry tournament in 1232 by Shunzei's Daughter[3] – later included as poem 32 in the *Shinshui wakashū* (New Collection of *Waka* Gleanings; 1364) – was regarded by Teika as a wonderful example of this poetic style:

> The morning frost
> sparkling on her sleeves,
> as the river wind at Uji
> sweeps through the mist –
> the Lady of the Bridge.

> *(Hashihime no / sode no asa-shimo / nao saete/
> kasumi fukikosu / Uji no kawa-kaze)*

The 'Lady of the Bridge' was a goddess who appears in legends, stories and poetry collections. She has several forms, including that of a lover waiting for a nightly visitor. Here, the haze and the morning frost imbue the romantic scene with ethereal beauty and elegance, and the poem is typical of the way that *yōen* celebrates fleeting and dream-like encounters portrayed in a mysterious atmosphere. Other characteristics of *yōen* include the sad or plaintive, the feminine, and subtle allusions to classical Chinese and Japanese stories that give the poems 'tale-like' qualities or the sense of being a scene taken from a drama.

Poems in the *yōen* style tend to be rich in imagery, with multiple, striking images compressed within a few lines, resulting in incredibly rich, layered verse. Teika's interest in love poetry is also related to his advocacy of the *yōen* style. Nevertheless, while the concept of *yōen* certainly influenced Teika's selection and interpretation of the poems in this collection, to what extent is difficult to establish definitively.

Later in life, Teika is said to have preferred a new stylistic ideal, *ushin* (conviction of feeling), a starker style favouring greater immediacy and intensity of passion over remote beauty. It was said to be an excellent vehicle for expressing difficulties in love, of which poem 89 is a fine example:

> Should I live longer
> I could not bear this secret love.
> Jewelled thread of life,
> since you must break –
> let it be now.

Ushin was also favoured for giving voice to the tribulations of life in general, as exemplified by poem 84:

> Since I now recall fondly
> the painful days of the past,
> if I live long, I may look back
> on these harsh days, too,
> and find them sweet and good.

Indeed, it seems fair to say that the majority of the poems in this collection are far removed in style from the bold experimentalism of the *yōen* and reflect Teika's later preference for a more sober, controlled approach.

Fujiwara no Teika has always been synonymous with Japanese high culture and *waka*, its most acclaimed literary genre, and there were many literary and artistic reinventions of his poetry and poetics in later periods, most notably at the end of the sixteenth and early seventeenth centuries. For example, the samurai warlord Hosokawa Yusai (1534–1610) and his disciple Karasumaru Mitsuhiro (1579–1638) revered him and took his poetic treatises as the foundation for their own poetry. Great calligraphers such as Hon'ami Koetsu (1558–1637) created stunning visual interpretations of Teika's poems about birds and flowers. Fragments of his idiosyncratic calligraphy were sought after by tea-ceremony aficionados, and hung in their tea rooms to invoke the spirit of elegance and refinement he represented. Today, Teika is still regarded as one of the greatest of Japanese literary figures and editors.

Understanding *Waka* and its Rhetorical Techniques

All of the poems in the *One Hundred Poets* are *waka*, the most ancient and prestigious of the traditional poetry genres. *Waka* serves as a general term for classical Japanese poetry in all its forms – except *renga* (linked verse) and *haiku* – as opposed to foreign verse, especially Chinese poetry. However, in the more usual, restricted sense, *waka* designates Japanese poetic forms pre-dating *renga* and *haiku*, namely *chōka*, *sedōka* and especially the thirty-one-syllable *tanka*. Since the Meiji period (1868–1912), the ancient term *tanka* has been revived and the form updated, replacing *waka* as the preferred term for poems in the classical thirty-one-syllable form. The poems are arranged in five lines in an alternating pattern of 5-7-5-7-7 syllables. In this volume, the majority of the translations are accordingly laid out over five lines.

Since early times, it was common practice to collect *waka* in large anthologies (*kashū*). The first extant *waka* anthology is the *Man'yōshū* (Collection of Ten Thousand Leaves; *c.*770). In the early tenth century, the first imperially commissioned anthology, the *Kokinshū*, was compiled. Imperial sponsorship made *waka* a highly prestigious genre, a status that it retained for a thousand years until the modern period. The tradition of compiling selections of poems by famous poets (*shūkasen*) began in the early eleventh century with Fujiwara no Kinto (966–1041; see poem 55), whose *Sanjūrokuninsen* (Selected Verse of Thirty-Six Poets; *c.*1009–12) can be considered the first work of this kind. By the time of Teika's *One Hundred Poets* (1230–40), the tradition was well established.

Like all genres, *waka* has its own rules and conventions, a knowledge of which allows for a deeper appreciation of the poems. When translated, some of the poems seem to be saying very little, but the originals often rely on a masterful use of rhetorical expression – especially wordplay and punning – to make them linguistically complex and aurally pleasing. For Heian-period poets, this enabled them both to demonstrate their mastery of the genre and to delight their readers. Notable rhetorical devices include literary puns (*kakekotoba*); prefaces (*jokotoba*), where an initial segment of a poem serves as a 'preface' to a word introduced later in the poem; associative words (*engo*), clusters of semantically related words embedded within a poem; and pillow words (*makura kotoba*), epithets used as conventional embellishments for certain words, 'raging' (*chi-hayaburu*) being often paired with 'gods' (*kami*), for example. An explanation of the main rhetorical techniques and some of the poetic forms is provided in the Glossary, while usage in specific poems is discussed in the Commentary.

Comparison with the *Hyakunin shūka*

Although the exact circumstances of the compilation of the *One Hundred Poets* are unknown, some facts are well established. In 1235 Teika was asked by his son's father-in-law, Utsunomiya Rensho (or Yoritsuna), to select a hundred poems to appear on the sliding doors of his country villa on Mount Ogura, west of Kyoto. An extant work known as *Hyakunin shūka* (Superior Poems by One Hundred Poets; 1229–36?) is thought to represent the original selection of poems that Teika gave to Rensho, although it is not known whether this pre-dates the *One Hundred Poets*. The poems were to be copied on squares of fine stiff paper (*shikishi*) and affixed to the doors of the villa, possibly accompanied by paintings.

There are several differences between the two works. Firstly, the *Hyakunin shūka* contains 101 poems instead of a hundred, leading some scholars to conjecture that Teika initially did not include one of his own poems in the selection out of modesty, but eventually was forced to do so by Rensho, driving the total number of poems up to 101. Furthermore, the poem by Minamoto no Toshiyori (no. 74 in the *One Hundred Poets*) is different in the *Hyakunin shūka*, while three poets who appear in the *Hyakunin shūka* (Emperor Ichijo's consort Teishi, Minamoto no Kunizane and Fujiwara no Nagakata) do not appear in the *One Hundred Poets* and are replaced by emperors Gotoba (poem 99) and Juntoku (poem 100). This has generated much debate. One view is that Gotoba and his son Juntoku were initially excluded from the selection for political reasons: they had rebelled against the shogunate in the Jokyu rebellion of 1221 and, as a consequence, Gotoba had been exiled to the Oki Islands and Juntoku to Sado Island. Teika included them in the selection at a later date when he felt comfortable enough to do so. Another possibility is that the *One Hundred Poets* may in fact pre-date the *Hyakunin shūka*, and that Gotoba and Juntoku were removed from the list after being initially included, again for political reasons. It is also possible that changes to an earlier version of the collection were made by someone other than Teika after his death, possibly his son Tameie and possibly at Teika's request. One of the main reasons supporting this conjecture is that the emperors Juntoku and Gotoba are referred to in the text as *in* (retired emperors), a title that they acquired only after Teika's death. Similarly, in the current version of the *One Hundred Poets* the poet Ietaka (poem 98) is referred to as Ietaka of the Junior Second Rank, but he only reached that rank after the date Teika himself recorded compiling the collection. Because so much about the details of compilation remains uncertain, it is difficult to make definitive claims regarding the formative process of the work.

Editorial Principles and Prominent Themes

Though the poems can be read and enjoyed with no background knowledge, a few details of the political context and culture are worth mentioning, along with Teika's principles for selecting, interpreting and arranging poems. These include the theory of 'association and progression' in the establishment of the poetic unity of the text; Teika's aesthetics and his predilection for love poetry; and his use of imagery.

It is no exaggeration to say that association is a central preoccupation of Japanese culture, both traditional and modern. An important idea in Japanese society is that of connection – embodied in the concept of *en* – and having a connection with someone or something is thought to be special and desirable. It is a fundamental element in the tea ceremony, for instance, where a tea utensil will be associated with the hanging scroll (such as cherry blossoms appearing on the tea bowl and in a poem on the scroll) and in poetry, where word association triggers internal resonances and creates verbal play. Because the Japanese language has countless homonyms, punning and word association are very easy to achieve. They constitute the basis of *rakugo*, a popular form of storytelling, in which wordplay provides a great part of the comic effect. Wordplay and word association are still important ingredients in many forms of contemporary culture, such as advertising and *manzai* (traditional stand-up) comedy.

Anthologies of Japanese court poetry often display a high degree of internal organization. In an influential article, Konishi Jin'ichi argued that the principles of progression and association were the main editorial techniques employed to create unity within an anthology.[4] Progression, in this context, might refer to the passing of time represented by the changing seasons, the cycle of court calendar events or the movement of a love affair from initial longing and brief fulfilment to betrayal and despair. Association may consist of grouping poems according to interrelated themes, such as, for example, poems invoking the same place name (Yoshino, Naniwa, etc.), dealing with the same topic (such as the coldness of dawn partings) or employing the same or similar imagery and diction.

Given that Teika was considered one of the editorial geniuses of his age, one would expect the *One Hundred Poets* to display strong principles of unity. It is true that there is a great deal of wordplay and association in the collection; however, it is not as coherently organized as some *waka* anthologies. Though some continuity between the various poems exists, the two main principles that seem to have guided Teika are chronological succession and the quality of the individual poems. This lack of internal structure and regularity is evident from a consideration of the main poetic categories (*budate*), as employed in imperial *waka* anthologies, that appear in the collection (see table opposite).[5]

CATEGORY	NUMBER OF POEMS	POEM NOS.
Spring	6	9, 15, 33, 35, 61, 73
Summer	4	2, 36, 81, 98
Autumn	15	1, 5, 17, 22, 23, 29, 32, 37, 47, 69, 70, 71, 79, 87, 94
Winter	6	4, 6, 28, 31, 64, 78
Travel	4	7, 11, 24, 93
Parting	1	16
Love	46	3, 13, 14, 18, 19, 20, 21, 25, 27, 30, 38, 39, 40, 41, 42, 43, 44, 45, 46, 48, 49, 50, 51, 52, 53, 54, 56, 58, 59, 62, 63, 65, 67, 72, 74, 77, 80, 82, 85, 86, 88, 89, 90, 91, 92, 97
Miscellaneous	18	8, 10, 12, 26, 34, 55, 57, 60, 66, 68, 75, 76, 83, 84, 95, 96, 99, 100

As the table shows, poems in one category are not always grouped together but may be interspersed throughout the collection. Nevertheless, a measure of unity is achieved by placing poems with common themes, imagery or diction together or near each other. Examples include autumn (poems 22 and 23), the dawn (30 and 31), hidden love (39–41), night (67–68), dusk (70–71), water (90, 92–93), robes and sleeves (90–92 and 93–94). And there are two large clusters of poems (38–46 and 48–54), all of which deal with love. This was clearly Teika's favourite theme, featuring in a great many of the poems.

In Teika's *Kindai shūka*, the arrangement of the poems is marked by his predilection for love poetry, especially the darker aspects of love, such as betrayal, abandonment, bitterness and despair. The same is certainly true of the *One Hundred Poets*,

whose treatment of love tends to focus on its more sombre, un-
happy aspects, though in a sense this is true of all *waka* poetry,
which does not celebrate happy or fulfilled love. Teika's under-
standing of poetic love was influenced by the poem-tale collection
The Tales of Ise (*Ise monogatari*; mid tenth century) and the ro-
mance novel *The Tale of Genji* (*Genji monogatari*; early eleventh
century), works which built on the tradition of poetic love and
eventually became themselves a central part of it. Both Teika and
his father regarded these works as mandatory reading for poets.

   Along with love, nature is especially prominent in the collec-
tion. As the table shows, autumn was a particularly popular
theme, with poems on this season greatly outnumbering those
on spring (fifteen, compared to six) and a scene of autumnal
melancholia opens the collection. The autumn poems almost
invariably paint a forlorn, melancholic image of the season, as
in poems 5, 23 and 47. Important exceptions are poems 17 and
69, by Narihira and Noin respectively, which focus on the stun-
ning beauty of the autumnal foliage. Rather than being a
matter of individual taste, the emphasis on desolate, melan-
cholic autumnal scenes was characteristic of the period in
which Teika lived – a troubled time of warfare and profound
political and social change. Beauty and sadness do not exclude
one another in the collection, but work together to create a pic-
ture of restrained elegance.

   Two of the defining metaphors of Japanese classical poetry
are the cherry blossom and maple. More than any other plants,
cherry blossoms and maples embody the strong love of the
Japanese for the four seasons, especially spring and autumn.
Whereas maples are celebrated mostly for their beauty, the
cherry blossom is more commonly associated with the evanes-
cence of life. This beautiful poem on cherry blossoms by Ki no
Tomonori (poem 33) hints at the profound way in which the
short-lived blossoms moved the early poets:

                     Cherry Blossoms,
                     on this calm, lambent

> day of spring,
> why do you scatter
> with such unquiet hearts?

The poet finds in the exquisite disquiet of the blossoms a mirror image of himself. The address to the cherry blossoms by Gyoson (poem 66), meanwhile, suggests that only they can fully understand the fragility of life:

> Mountain Cherry,
> let us console each other.
> Of all those I know
> no one understands my heart
> the way your blossoms do.

Though maples are also short-lived, it is their visual beauty that is mostly celebrated, often in connection with the gods or the imperial family. For example, Sugawara no Michizane's charming poem (no. 24) asks the gods to accept a maple brocade instead of the streamers that were usually offered:

> On this journey
> I have no streamers to offer up.
> Instead, dear gods, if it pleases you,
> may you take this maple brocade
> of Mount Tamuke's colours.

In poem 26, Fujiwara no Tadahira asks the maples of Mount Ogura to wait for the progess of the Daigo emperor so that he may see them in all their autumn finery:

> Dear Maples of Mount Ogura,
> if you have a heart,
> please wait for another visit
> so that His Majesty may enjoy
> your lovely autumn colours.

Elsewhere maple leaves are associated with images of cloth, such as the famous brocades and tie-dyeing of poem 17.

What many of the poems focusing on the natural world have in common is a celebration of the beauty of a single observed moment and an emphasis on the importance of the ability to be moved by it. This was a key characteristic of Japanese classical poetry, and the harnessing of this sensibility was later important in the creation of *haiku*, where the lens becomes even more microscope-like. Poem 93 is a good example of a verse that is affecting because of its precise, sharp focus on a single image:

> That such moving sights
> would never change –
> fishermen rowing
> their small boats,
> pulling them on to shore.

In contrast, the poem on Mount Fuji, by Yamabe no Akahito (no. 4), is a notable exception in the collection in its celebration of the majesty and monumentality of the landscape:

> Coming out on the Bay of Tago
> there before me,
> Mount Fuji –
> snow still falling on her peak,
> a splendid cloak of white.

The 'splendid cloak' of Mount Fuji provides a good opportunity to mention what was clearly Teika's favourite colour: white – referred to in poems 2, 4, 6, 15, 29, 31, 37 and 76. Just as we speak of 'Rikyu grey' in the Japanese tea ceremony or of 'Issey Miyake black' in contemporary Japanese fashion, for Teika – and for the Japanese aesthetic sensibility more generally – white was the colour of refinement, purity, elegance and sophistication. White is also a key element of Teika's *yōen* aesthetics.

Poems in this style often feature natural scenes in white or pale colours, such as the white moon of dawn, cherry blossoms, fog, mist and snow. There are at least ten poems in the collection that employ white imagery, including poem 2:

> Spring has passed
> and the white robes of summer
> are being aired
> on fragrant Mount Kagu –
> beloved of the gods.

Here, whiteness is associated both with summer and the sacred gods of old. White can be used for autumn and winter too, as in poem 37, which compares white dewdrops to unstrung pearls:

> When the wind gusts
> over the autumn fields,
> white dewdrops
> lie strewn about
> like scattered pearls.

Some of the best poems in the collection involve a kind of 'elegant confusion' (*mitate*) on the part of the onlooker by the appearance of white on white. Poem 76 describes the poet's inability to distinguish between white waves and far-off clouds, while in poem 31 Sakanoue no Korenori confuses the snow with moonlight. Poem 96 humorously compares white blossoms to snow, only to reveal that in fact the whiteness is the white hair of old age. In poem 29 – one of the most beautiful in the collection and a favourite of Teika's that he included in several other compilations – Oshikochi no Mitsune writes of his inability to pluck white chrysanthemums because they are indistinguishable from the first frost:

> To pluck a stem
> I shall have to guess,

> for I cannot tell apart
> white chrysanthemums
> from the first frost.

This recurrence of white imagery is related to the aesthetic idea of *setsugekka* (literally, 'snow, moon and flowers'). Originally a phrase in a poem by the Chinese poet Bai Juyi (772–846), it gradually developed into an important motif in Japanese poetry and art. Bai wrote to his friend the scholar Yuan Zhen that he missed him most when he saw the blossoms blooming, the moon at night and the snow in winter. All three of these are associated with the colour white, and white in turn came to be loved by the Japanese classical poets. The poems in *One Hundred Poets* reveal how central the colour was to Teika's aesthetic and how widely it was employed in the poetry of the time.

One additional characteristic of the collection particularly worth noting is the strikingly visual evocation of landscape and specific places. Perhaps Teika envisaged that illustrations would be later added to the poems, and so he deliberately chose intensely visual poems that lent themselves well to such use. Or maybe it was just a consequence of his own personal preference for poems with vivid pictorial imagery. Regardless, the *One Hundred Poets* is a highly visual anthology.

Famous locations referred to in Japanese classical poetry are known as *utamakura* (literally, 'poem pillows') and have been highly popular since early times. They carried a convenient range of established associations that poets used to add wit and depth to their verse. Places such as Naniwa, the Osaka Barrier, Tatsuta and Yoshino also carried political and cultural significance. (See the Glossary entry on *utamakura* for a list of the famous sites that crop up repeatedly in the poems.)

Related to this emphasis on the visual is ekphrasis – poems about paintings or visual images or the combination of visual and literary depiction – which is an important element in the *One Hundred Poets*. Indeed, Japanese literature as a whole is intensely ekphratic because of the recurring tendency to pair

poems and excerpts from works in prose with visual depictions
in a great variety of media and genres. Examples include the
poem-painting scrolls (*shigajiku*) of the Muromachi period
(1336–1573) and the outstanding lacquerware of the Momoy-
ama and Edo periods (1574–1868). In Japan, poems and
paintings have been regularly paired since at least the Heian
period (794–1185).

One of the most common ways of pairing poem and picture
was through 'screen poems' (*byōbu-uta*), in which poets based
their compositions on images depicted on partition screens
(*byōbu*), rather than on scenes from the real world, and word
and image worked as an integral whole. In some cases, poets
imagined themselves as figures in the painting and composed
from that viewpoint. There are several theories as to how the
poems were placed on the screens. One is that a space was left
blank on the screens and the poems were written directly on to
the screen; another is that the poems were written on a piece of
paper and then affixed to the screen near the image. The land-
scape described in the poems is not always nature in its primal
state; sometimes it may be an aristocrat's manmade garden –
the most famous being that of Minamoto no Toru – and other
times the painted scene itself. In this collection, poem 17 by
Narihira and poem 98 by Ietaka were specifically composed for
partition screens. (See commentary to both these poems for
further detail.)

Connection to the Imperial Family

An important aspect of the *One Hundred Poets* is its close con-
nection to the imperial family and noble families of the court.
Poetry composition and literary patronage have been essential
activities of the imperial family for more than a millennium,
and imperial patronage in turn has played a crucial role in the
development of Japanese court poetry. In Teika's world, lineage,
status at court and poetic ability were all inseparable. The *One*

Hundred Poets closely reflects this and can be seen as an encomium to the imperial institution. It is clear from reading the collection that, for Teika, in addition to being accomplished composers, imperials were also the spiritual patrons of *waka*; the collection opens and closes with poems by sovereigns (Emperor Tenji and Empress Jito at the beginning, and emperors Gotoba and Juntoku at the end). Emperor Tenji was Jito's father and Gotoba was Juntoku's father, so by placing them at each end of the collection, Teika is affirming both the centrality of the imperial family to poetry and the importance of heredity and lineage.

The *One Hundred Poets* covers almost six centuries of Japanese history, from the reign of Emperor Tenji (r. 661–72) to Emperor Juntoku (r. 1211–21). The thirty-eighth emperor, Tenji, whose *waka* opens the volume, was not only the first emperor for whom a reliable historical record remains, but also the sovereign who first ennobled the Fujiwara family and gave it its illustrious clan name. Thus, the first poem simultaneously celebrates the imperial line, the beginning of *waka* and the beginning of the Fujiwara family. In his general layout of the *One Hundred Poets*, Teika can be seen to acknowledge a deep family debt to Tenji and his descendants. Emperor Tenji was a great patron of poets and poetry and was himself an accomplished poet. He was the first to establish the close links between the imperial court and the world of poetry that are faithfully fostered to this day.

The second poet to appear in the *One Hundred Poets* is Tenji's daughter Jito (r. 686–97), an empress who carried on her father's patronage of poets and poetry. No doubt her inclusion in the *One Hundred Poets* is owing to her importance as a patron of poetry. She is especially noteworthy for her patronage of the great early poet Kakinomoto no Hitomaro (*fl.* late seventh century), who is the collection's third poet. Since, as early as the tenth century, Hitomaro was revered as a deity of poetry, the collection would have probably opened with him, had Teika not wished to give precedence to poets from the imperial family. Hitomaro regarded Jito as a goddess in a way no other later poet regarded members of the imperial family, so his inclusion following two rulers may be seen as a tribute to him by Teika. The *One Hundred Poets* closes with Emperor Juntoku, preceded by his father Emperor Gotoba. Gotoba is himself preceded by Fujiwara no Ietaka, a fine poet and known for his unswerving loyalty to his sovereign even after his banishment to Oki Island. The great link between them was poetry.

The remaining four emperors in the collection, Koko, Sanjo, Sutoku and Yozei, were chosen for their significance in the world of poetry. For example, Emperor Yozei (r. 876–84; poem 13), the fifty-seventh sovereign, came to the throne in childhood, but he was deposed after a mere eight years of reign because he showed signs of mental instability. After his abdication, he became an assiduous practitioner of poetry and a host of poetic contests. Regrettably, only one of his poems remains extant – the one in the *One Hundred Poets*.

As well as the eight emperors, there are four children of emperors (including Princess Shokushi), four grandsons of emperors and two great-grandsons. There are twenty-five named Fujiwaras, as well as priests or women who were of Fujiwara stock. There are many pairs of parent and child (poems 1 and 2, 12 and 21, 13 and 20, 25 and 44, 30 and 41, 40 and 59, 42 and 62, 45 and 50, 55 and 64, 56 and 60, 57 and 58, 71 and 74, 74 and 85, 76 and 95, 79 and 84, 83 and 87, 83 and 97, 99 and 100), and one pair of brothers (16 and 17). Teika lived in an age when descent from a family of poets was of the utmost importance, and he himself was the head of one of the most important houses of poetry (the Mikohidari house). This, then, is a thoroughly blue-blooded, elitist and exclusive group.

Nevertheless, it is important to understand that Teika was not simply practising family favouritism. It is unsurprising that so many members of the Fujiwara clan are included, given that it produced so many outstanding poets. Furthermore, Teika clearly wanted to pay tribute to others who had compiled selections of great poetry before him. Notable is his inclusion of twenty-five of the thirty-six reputed poets that his distant ancestor Fujiwara no

Kinto (see poem 55) included in his *Sanjūrokuninsen* (Selected Poems by Thirty-Six Poets; 1009–11?), an important precursor of the *One Hundred Poets*. It also evident that he chose some poets for their historical importance, rather than for the beauty of their poems. For example, Teika did not include poems 13, 25, 50 and 55 (by Yozei, Fujiwara no Sadakata, Fujiwara no Yoshitaka and Kinto respectively) in any other of the numerous selections of excellent examples that he compiled in his lifetime. He included them here because these poets represented important stages in the history and development of *waka*.

Waka poetry continued to be written throughout the centuries, and in 1879 the Emperor Meiji (r. 1868–1912) opened the *utakai hajime* New Year Poetry Reading Ceremony – an annual *waka* contest held at the palace based on a topic chosen by the Imperial Household Agency – to the general public. Today, the contest welcomes *waka* submissions from commoners all over Japan and overseas and even from non-Japanese, and the tie between *waka* and the imperial family remains strong. All members of the imperial family still continue to write *waka* throughout the year and their *waka* are read at the ceremony, along with ten *waka* selected from contributions by the general public. The reading is held as part of the New Year celebrations at the palace. The present empress, Michiko, is an excellent poet, as is her daughter, Sayako Kuroda.

Poems by Women

There were many outstanding female poets in Heian times and this is reflected in the number of poems by women in the collection. Apart from Jito, who was an empress, there are twenty women, many of them ladies-in-waiting to imperial consorts. The most rhetorically complicated and emotionally intense poems in this collection are mostly by women. Poems 60 and 62 are especially impressive, as is no. 9, by Ono no Komachi (*fl.* mid ninth century):

> I have loved in vain
> and now my beauty fades
> like these cherry blossoms
> paling in the long rains of spring
> that I gaze out upon alone.

The poem is striking for its technical brilliance: almost every word is embroidered with many layers of meaning. Many commentators have written of it as the *cri de coeur* of an old woman who was in her heyday a very great beauty, blessed with exceptional talent, sensually alive, and feted and loved by many. Now her beauty has faded, her lovers are dead or gone, and her poetic talent is weakening. I do not disagree with this interpretation, but additional considerations must also be taken into account. Ono no Komachi is like many Japanese women of talent. In Japanese culture, women have traditionally taken roles subservient to men, which has meant that they have had less freedom and have had to overcome greater challenges in expressing themselves. One of the principal modes of expression employed by women was negation. When praised, the first response was (and to some extent still is) to negate. In this poem, Ono no Komachi employs the classical device of negation to produce what is ostensibly a lament for her fading beauty and talents. But it is important to see what the poem affirms. It is hard to imagine that Komachi was unaware of her achievement and stature as a poet. In other words, the poet is saying something like: 'Yes, I am growing old and am less beautiful than I once was. Maybe you superficial (especially male!) readers will no longer find me attractive, but if you have a minimum of discernment, you will be able to see under my disguise and realize that the sadness of life has only sharpened my genius. Fade away, those of you who can only see the surface; and even those of you who can see beyond the surface, approach gingerly, for the profundity of my emotion has made me as formidable as ever.' (See the Note on the Translation for further discussion of this poem.)

Conclusion

One of the great strengths of classical Japanese *waka* poetry is that it can express deep emotion and refinement of sensibility in images of profound simplicity, and the *One Hundred Poets* is an exemplary work in this regard. Its poems contain rich and original images that still seem fresh a thousand years later. The collection shows how Teika defined himself in relation to the poetic tradition that he both inherited and promulgated. According to Emperor Gotoba, Teika was dictatorial in all matters relating to poetry and editing, but eight hundred years of history have consistently proved his judgements right.

Although it is impossible to state unequivocally the work's overarching editorial principles, this should not become a hindrance to the appreciation of the individual poems. The *One Hundred Poets* remains first and foremost a collection of one hundred great poems and so it should be regarded. The primary aim in this book is to provide an enjoyable and poetic translation, and I hope that readers will find in these pages something of the depth and beauty of the original magical collection, which is notable for the great subtlety and allusiveness of the poems, their incomparable visual imagery and the profound emotion that they express.

Haiku is widely known in the West, but it originally developed from *waka*. *Haiku*, a relatively recent word, was originally known as *hokku* and was the opening stanza in Japanese linked verse, *renga*. *Haiku* came into being when the opening stanza came to exist independently from the rest of the linked verse. Formally, it is the equivalent of the upper strophe of *waka*, namely having seventeen syllables of 5-7-5. Though *haiku* developed in a completely different way to *waka*, a study of Japanese *waka* can help readers in understanding more about *haiku* and how to write it. When Shunzei noted, 'All who come to our land study this poetry; all who live in our land compose it', he was speaking of *waka* not *haiku*.[6] Thus, if one wants to understand the heart of the Japanese it could be argued that it is found not only in *haiku*, but also – or even more – in *waka*.

Towards the end of working on this translation, I accompanied the translator and scholar Eileen Kato on a pilgrimage to Kyoto to visit places connected with *One Hundred Poets*. We visited the ruins of the legendary Shiguretei in Nisonin, where Teika is said to have completed his editing of the collection in the little hut at the foot of Mount Ogura, which gave the work the name by which it is commonly known in Japan, the *Ogura hyakunin isshu*. We also visited the site of what is held to be the grave of Teika in Shokukuji. He lies alongside two other great figures, the Muromachi patron of the arts Ashikaga Yoshimasa (1436–90) and the artist Ito Jakuchu (1716–1800). We placed a small bunch of white chrysanthemums on the grave in honour of Teika's love of the colour white. At the time, I remember thinking of the extraordinary power of literature. More than six centuries after the death of Teika, two people from the other side of the world more than six thousand miles away were paying homage to this outstanding poet and editor. Great literature knows no barriers in time or distance. I hope the readers of this translation will gain a sense of the power and beauty of these poems and even be moved to return to the originals. And, as I happily discovered myself, I can end with one recommendation: if you want to understand the Japanese, read the *One Hundred Poets*.

NOTES

1.   The card game consists of two hundred cards divided into two sets, one with the complete poems, which are called the *yomifuda* (cards to be read out), and one with only the last lines of the poems, the *torifuda* (cards to grab), which are placed face up on the card table. When the *yomifuda* are read out, the players have to find the *torifuda* with the last lines of the relevant poems as quickly as possible and snap them up. The person with the most cards at the end is the winner. The game has been played since the Edo period, and is still played every New Year by around a

million people in Japan. At the time of writing, I am also creating the world's first English-language version of the card game, with the tentative title of *Whack a Waka*. Indeed, one of the motivations behind the creation of the new translation of the poems – with five lines each – was to make a version suitable for the card game.

2. Teika quoted this himself in his revised *Shūigusō* (Dull Musings of a Chamberlain; written after 1216): 'Everyone said I wrote "faddish, groundless Zen-nonsense poems" and abandoned me.'

3. Known as 'Shunzei's Daughter', she was in fact Shunzei's grand-daughter and therefore Teika's niece.

4. Konishi Jin'ichi, 'Association and Progression: Principles of Integration in Anthologies and Sequences of Japanese Court Poetry, A.D. 900–1350', *Harvard Journal of Asiatic Studies*, vol. 21 (December 1958), pp. 67–127.

5. The table here is just to give a general idea of the main poetic categories and their distribution throughout the collection. Precise categorization of the poems is a matter of debate. For example, the number of love poems varies depending on whether we count them as they were originally categorized or whether we simply judge them to be love poems from a Western point of view. And some poems can belong to two categories simultaneously, such as poem 91, which, as the commentary to it indicates, was initially regarded as belonging to autumn, but which may also be counted as a love poem.

6. Shunzei, *Korai fūteishō* (1197–1201), a treatise on poetry writing and the history of *waka*. Adapted here from Eileen Kato (trans.), 'Pilgrimage to Dazaifu: Sōgi's *Tsukushi no Michi no Ki*', *Monumenta Nipponica*, vol. 34, no. 3 (Autumn 1979), pp. 333–67, at p. 364.

Further Reading

Under 'Works in Japanese', names appear in the Japanese order of family name followed by personal name.

Works in English

Atkins, Paul S., *Teika: The Life and Works of a Medieval Japanese Poet* (Honolulu: University of Hawai'i Press, 2017)

Bly, Robert, *The Eight Stages of Translation* (Boston, MA: Rowan Tree Press, 1986)

Bundy, Roselee, 'Solo Poetry Contest as Poetic Self-Portrait: The One-Hundred-Round Contest of Lord Teika's Own Poems': part 1, *Monumenta Nipponica*, vol. 61, no. 1 (Spring 2006), pp. 1–58; part 2, *Monumenta Nipponica*, vol. 61, no. 2 (Summer 2006), pp. 131–92

Cranston, Edwin A. (trans.), *A Waka Anthology*, vol. 2: *Grasses of Remembrance*, (Stanford, CA: Stanford University Press, 2006)

Fujiwara no Teika, *Fujiwara Teika's 'Superior Poems of Our Time': A Thirteenth-Century Poetic Treatise and Sequence*, trans. Robert H. Brower and Earl Miner (Stanford, CA: Stanford University Press, 1967)

——, *Muigetsushō*, trans. Toshihiko and Toyo Izutsu, in their *The Theory of Beauty in the Classical Aesthetics of Japan* (The Hague, Boston and London: Martinus Nijhoff Publishers, 1981), pp. 79–96

Kato, Eileen (trans.), 'Pilgrimage to Dazaifu: Sōgi's *Tsukushi no Michi no Ki*', *Monumenta Nipponica*, vol. 34, no. 3 (Autumn 1979), pp. 333–67

Keene, Donald, *Japanese Literature: An Introduction for Western Readers* (Tokyo: Charles E. Tuttle, 1977)

——, *The Pleasures of Japanese Literature* (New York: Columbia University Press, 1988)

——, *Seeds in the Heart: Japanese Literature from Earliest Times to the Late Sixteenth Century* (New York: Henry Holt, 1993)

Kenko, *Essays in Idleness: The Tsurezuregusa of Kenkō*, trans. Donald Keene (New York: Columbia University Press, 1967)

Konishi Jin'ichi, *A History of Japanese Literature*, vol. 3: *The High Middle Ages*, trans. Aileen Gatten and Mark Harbison (Princeton, NJ: Princeton University Press, 1991), pp. 214–16

MacMillan, Peter (trans. and ed.), *The Tales of Ise* (London: Penguin Books, 2016)

McCullough, Helen Craig, *Brocade by Night: 'Kokin Wakashū' and the Court Style in Japanese Classical Poetry* (Stanford, CA: Stanford University Press, 1985)

——(trans. and ed.), *Kokin Wakashū: The First Imperial Anthology of Japanese Poetry: With 'Tosa Nikki' and 'Shinsen Waka'* (Stanford, CA: Stanford University Press, 1985)

Miner, Earl, *An Introduction to Japanese Court Poetry* (Stanford, CA: Stanford University Press, 1968)

——, Hiroko Odagiri and Robert E. Morrell, *The Princeton Companion to Classical Japanese Literature* (Princeton, NJ: Princeton University Press, 1958)

Mostow, Joshua, *Pictures of the Heart* (Honolulu: University of Hawai'i Press, 1996)

Rexroth, Kenneth, *One Hundred Poems from the Japanese* (New York: New Directions, 1964)

Works in Japanese

Ariyoshi Tamotsu, *Hyakunin isshu* (Tokyo: Kōdansha, 1983)

Harashima Hiroshi, *Hyakunin isshu konjaku sanpo* (Tokyo: Chukei Shuppan, 2012)

Inoue Muneo, *Hyakunin isshu o tanoshiku yomu* (Tokyo: Kasama Shoin, 2002)

——, *Hyakunin isshu: Ōchō waka kara chūsei sekai e* (Tokyo: Kasama Shoin, 2004)

Katagiri Yōichi, *Utamakura utakotoba jiten* (Tokyo: Kasama Shoin, 1999)

Kubota Jun and Baba Akiko (eds), *Utakotoba utamakura daijiten* (Tokyo: Kadokawa Shoten, 1999)

Nakanishi Susumu, *Nakanishi Susumu to aruku Hyakunin isshu no Kyoto* (Kyoto: Kyoto Shinbun, 2007)

Oka Makoto, *Hyakunin isshu* (Tokyo: Sekai Bunkasha, 2005)

Shimaoka Shin, *Hyakunin isshu o aruku* (Tokyo: Kōfūsha, 1995)

Shimazu Tadao, *Hyakunin isshu*, 2nd edn (Tokyo: Kadokawa Shoten, 1999)

——and Kamijo Shoji (eds), *Hyakunin isshu kochū shō* (Osaka: Izumi Shoin, 1982)

Shirasu Masako, *Watashi no Hyakunin isshu* (Tokyo: Shinchōsha, 2005)

Shogaku Tosho Gengo Kenkyujo (eds), *Hyakunin isshu no techō: Kōrin karuta de yomu Hyakunin isshu* (Tokyo: Shogakukan, 1984)

Suzuki Hideo, Yamaguchi Shin'ichi and Yoda Yasushi, *Genshoku Ogura hyakunin isshu* (Tokyo: Bun'eidō, 2004)

Tani Tomoko, *Karā-ban Hyakunin isshu* (Tokyo: Kadokawa Gakugei Shuppan, 2013)

Note on the Translation

This translation is based on the second edition of Shimazu Tadao's *Hyakunin isshu* (Tokyo: Kadokawa Shoten, 1999). The first translation of the *Hyakunin isshu*, by Frederick Victor Dickins, was published in 1866 and since then there have been over a dozen translations of this work in English alone. The work poses many challenges to the translator. These include how to render the conventions of *waka* expression and the multiplicity of possible interpretations allowed by the poems; the treatment of punning and wordplay; the role of the subject marker; and other matters of form. One of the difficulties of translating the *Hyakunin isshu* is that classical Japanese is full of long-established conventions that are not always accessible to the modern reader. A number of common literary conventions are defined in the Glossary. One example is *utamakura* or famous place names with poetic associations and alternative meanings based upon the sound of a word. The place name Osaka, for example, was often used to signify a place of meeting, especially in the context of lovers, as the long *o* at the beginning of the word was written in the same way as *au* (to meet). The mere mention of the word would cause such associations to immediately spring to mind for the educated Japanese reader of old, but not for contemporary Japanese, much less for non-Japanese.

Another challenge is that, at times, the poets capture an extremely simple scene so subtly that, when translated, it can seem little more than a physical picture or part of a longer verse rather than a whole poem. Sometimes these poems have clever rhetorical features that buoy up the verse in Japanese, but it is not always possible to convey that in English. The simpler poems on the seasons are especially difficult to translate while preserving the poetic delicacy of the original.

Yet another challenge is the number of different interpretations that are possible. A classic example is poem 99. The word 'people' (*hito*) in the poem can be taken to mean different people, some of whom are amiable and some of whom are not, or the same people at different moments in time. Another possible interpretation is that there are many sides to a person, only some of which are agreeable. Here are some of the ways in which the last two lines of the Japanese can be interpreted:

> Some people are kind,
> while others are hateful.

> Some have been kind to me,
> while others were hateful.

> Sometimes people are kind,
> sometimes hateful.

> Sometimes I long for them,
> sometimes I just hate them.

While it is unusual for there to be such a variety of different interpretations, two or three distinct interpretations are often possible, posing a considerable challenge to the translator.

Another reason for such ambiguity is that, at the time Teika was editing the collection, some of the poems preceded him by as much as five hundred years, which means that they came to him with variants and historical shifts in nuance and meaning. The way Teika read the poems is not always the way the poems' original audience would have done. Poem 17 by Ariwara no Narihira is a good example:

Such beauty unheard of
even in the age of the raging gods –
the Tatsuta River
tie-dyeing its waters
in autumnal colours.

*(Chihayaburu / kamiyo mo kikazu / Tatsutagawa /
karakurenai ni / mizu kukuru to wa)*

Because in classical *kana* orthography there were no vocaliza-
tion marks, the last line of the poem can be read both as *mizu
kukuru to wa* ([the maple leaves] tie-dye the water) and *mizu kug-
uru to wa* (water streams below [the maples leaves]). It is fairly
certain that readers of the *Kokinshū*, from which Teika took the
poem, read it *kukuru* (to tie-dye), whereas Teika and his contem-
poraries almost certainly read it *kuguru* (to flow beneath). I have
generally tried to follow Teika's interpretation, but in this in-
stance I prefer the original reading.

In the following poem (no. 30), one possible interpretation is
that it is only the face of the moon that is cold, not the lover:

How cold the face
of the morning moon!
Since we parted
nothing is so miserable
as the approaching dawn.

Many scholars, however, think that 'cold' refers to both, in which
case the translation would be:

Since I parted from you,
nothing is so miserable
as that time before dawn,
the look on your face then
cold as the moon at dawn.

Such complications have meant that the Japanese invariably have read the *One Hundred Poets* with the aid of countless commentaries written since the thirteenth century. English translations, by contrast, have tended to include as few notes as possible, on the assumption that it should be possible to understand a poem simply by reading it and that knowing about the historical reception and background of a literary work is not essential. However, this edition includes a commentary, which I hope will contribute to a deeper understanding of the background and context within which the poems were written and increase the reader's enjoyment of the poems.

Japanese poetry avoids rhyme and depends more on rhythm (*onritsu*) than on metre, which is quantitative, not accentual. English free verse is thus a very natural choice when translating classical Japanese verse. Some believe that classical poetry as well as contemporary *tanka* – which uses the same form as classical *waka* – should be translated following the syllable count of *waka* and *tanka*, 5-7-5-7-7. According to this view, all translations of poems have the same number of syllables (thirty-one), but this makes for an unnatural and meaningless constriction in English. In order to give a sense of the *form* of the original, I have tended to use five lines for the poems. I have in general tried to stick as closely as possible to Teika's interpretation of the poems, but on a few occasions I have followed the interpretation of the poem when it first appeared in a different anthology.

The abundance of punning and wordplay is perhaps the biggest challenge for any translator. Where possible I have incorporated the wordplay and punning of the original, which are all outlined in the Commentary. It should be noted, however, that whereas in English punning is seen as a form of light and sometimes naive wordplay, in classical Japanese it was admired as an expression of the poet's skill. Unlike English, there are countless homonyms in Japanese, making punning very easy, but it is challenging to think of puns that could work in English for the numerous Japanese counterparts. Moreover, punning and wordplay of this kind is not popular in English poetry today, except for nonsense verse or children's poems, so even in those rare circumstances when it is possible to convey the pun, it may not always be appreciated by adult readers of English poetry, so the translator is always torn as to how much one can reproduce puns without sounding bathetic. Incidentally, there is only one poem, no. 16, that happens to convey the same pun in both languages, based on the Japanese word *matsu*, which means both a pine tree and to pine for someone, as the word 'pine' does in English:

> Though I may leave
> for Mount Inaba,
> whose peak is covered with **pines**,
> if I hear that you **pine** for me,
> I will come straight home to you.

Should imagery in Japanese traditional poetry be translated as similes or metaphors? Translations into modern Japanese in the contemporary commentaries tend to interpret the images as similes using the words *yō* or *no gotoku* ('like' or 'as'). In the original, however, this information was often only implied, because the number of syllables was predetermined, and it was not always possible to include all grammatical information. Although the words for 'like' and 'as' are not explicit in the poem, it does not mean that they are not part of the meaning. Nor does it mean that the image should instead be interpreted as a metaphor. It is often preferable to translate such images as similes rather than metaphors, because similes are not as forceful as metaphors and are in keeping with the love of indirection that informs Japanese poetry. In some cases, however, a metaphor is preferable. The criterion I used in choosing between them was which would read best as a poem in English.

Many of the poems in this collection are highly visual, such as poem 3, for which I decided to do a word-picture translation:

The
long
tail
of
the
copper
pheasant
trails,
drags
on
and
on
like
this
long
night
alone
in
the
lonely
mountains,
longing
for
my
love.

The poet compares a long night spent alone to the long tail of
the copper pheasant, and the translation is intended to convey
visually the length of the tail. In the original, certain sounds are
repeated, especially *na* and *o*, replicated in the translation by
the repetition of 'o' and 'n' in words such as 'on and on', 'alone'
and 'longing', to create a similar effect and make the night seem
longer.

    Another important issue in classical, and contemporary,
Japanese is that the subject marker (such as 'I' for the speaker in
a poem) is often left out, which means that when translating

one would naturally use the passive rather than the active voice. In poem 5, for example, two different readings are possible depending on whether one takes as the subject of 'making a path through the fallen leaves' to be the deer or the poet, and this is part of the pleasure of reading such poems. For the main translation, I have used the passive voice without a subject marker, as in the original poem. If the subject marker is included, the translation might read:

> Rustling through the leaves,
> going deep into the mountains,
> when I hear the lonely deer
> belling for his doe,
> how forlorn the autumn feels.

The Japanese language allows for much ambiguity, hence the absence of the subject marker does not necessarily mean that the poet wanted the reader to think it was either the deer or the poet that was moving forth into the woods, but rather to allow for the possibility of both interpretations. Not to clearly identify the subject in an English poem causes confusion, however, so in the main text I have tended to give a translation that follows the demands of English grammar, placing the more ambiguous version in the Commentary, where relevant. Such ambiguity in linguistic expression is one of the beauties and strengths of classical and even contemporary Japanese and is a special feature of *waka* poetry, perhaps reflecting the sensibility of poets whose relationship with nature is closer and more integrated, unlike their Western counterparts, who traditionally stand divorced and in opposition to nature.

A closer consideration of one poem, Ono no Komachi's masterful no. 9 (see also the Introduction, p. xxix), will exemplify some of the issues outlined here:

> I have loved in vain
> and now my beauty fades

like these cherry blossoms
paling in the long rains of spring
that I gaze out upon alone.

(Hana no iro wa / utsurinikerina / itazurani /
waga mi yo ni furu / nagame seshi ma ni)

In this extraordinarily dense poem, brilliantly conveyed in the thirty-two syllables of the original Japanese, almost every word has two or more meanings, some of which are listed below:

hana means '(cherry) blossoms', but also 'art'.
iro means both 'colour' and 'sexuality/sensuality'.
utsuru (the infinitive of *utsurinikeri*) is to 'pale', 'fade', 'change' or 'scatter'.
itazura ni means 'in vain', 'come to nothing' and 'meaningless time passed by'. In the poem, it functions as pivot phrase (see commentary to poem 9) that modifies both what precedes and what follows it, helping to convey the overall sense that peerless beauty and youth and talent and love were all in vain.
waga mi yo ni furu means 'I grow old', 'as I idled away' and 'I have (many) romantic relationships'.
yo means 'world', 'life' and 'romantic/sexual relationship'.
furu means 'to grow old', 'falling rain' and 'to pass through life'.
nagame means 'lost in thought', 'long rains' and 'gaze upon'.
furu nagame is the 'endless-falling rain', the end of this phrase overlapping the following one: *nagame seshi ma ni* (literally, 'while I gaze at it').

Because of the polysemy, the first two lines, *Hana no iro wa / utsurinikeri na*, have two distinct and quite clear meanings:

(1) The literal meaning that the cherry blossoms are faded.
(2) The metaphorical meaning that the beautiful woman's (*hana no*) charms, beauty and sensuality are gone.

At its simplest level, the poem can be read as a description of the blossoms blooming in vain and scattering in the prolonged rains, but from line 3 onwards, this seasonal imagery is super-imposed on a narrative of personal decline. It is impossible to capture in English all of the nuances of the original without seeming terribly overloaded, but the many exclusions that are necessary mean that the translation conveys only part of the rich, suggestive quality of the original. Not only is there the problem of translating all of the plurality of meanings, there is also the problem of conveying what is unsaid.

If I were to compare poetry and translation to the visual arts, I would say that poetry writing corresponds to abstract or fig-urative painting and translation corresponds to coloured woodblock printing. In poetry, one either writes freely in bold strokes (or at least gives that impression), as in abstract painting, or one uses venerable techniques to create figurative images that seem entirely fresh. In translating poetry, one may begin with a bold stroke to capture the essence of the poem, but then one has to keep returning to the original, each new application adding a different colour, as in the layering-up of a colour print. To execute the task properly, one must be methodical and pre-cise, for any error would mean a loss of colour, or application of colour to an unintended part of the surface. I cannot claim that this translation is as exact and faithful to the original as a print in which each colour is rigorously applied to the matrix until a complete image forms. Rather, I would describe it as a combin-ation of a painting and a print, not completely literal in every respect but faithful to the *heart* of the original. Teika himself advocated the imbuing of new sentiments into ancient words as a legitimate way of composing poems, and what better metaphor for the art of translation? Each new age has its own linguistic and emotional requirements but these energize rather than negate the process of translation.

A Note on Macrons

Macrons are used to extend vowel sounds in the romanized form of Japanese. I have tried to keep them to a minimum throughout this volume, omitting them from the names of people and places; exceptions are transliterated words and phrases in the editorial matter and in cases where it is part of the official English name of a company, such as the publishing firm Shinchōsha.

ONE HUNDRED POETS,
ONE POEM EACH

1. Emperor Tenji

In this makeshift hut
in the autumn field
gaps in the thatch
let dewdrops in,
moistening my sleeves.

2. *Empress Jito*

Spring has passed,
and the white robes of summer
are being aired
on fragrant Mount Kagu –
beloved of the gods.

3. Kakinomoto no Hitomaro

The
long
tail
of
the
copper
pheasant
trails,
drags
on
and
on
like
this
long
night
alone
in
the
lonely
mountains,
longing
for
my
love.

4. *Yamabe no Akahito*

Coming out on the Bay of Tago,
there before me,
Mount Fuji –
snow still falling on her peak,
a splendid cloak of white.

5. Sarumaru Taifu

In the deep mountains
making a path
through the fallen leaves,
the plaintive belling of the stag –
how forlorn the autumn feels.

6. Otomo no Yakamochi

How the night deepens.
A ribbon of the whitest frost
is stretched across
the bridge of magpie wings
the lovers will cross.

7. *Abe no Nakamaro*

I gaze up at the sky and wonder:
is that the same moon
that shone over Mount Mikasa
at Kasuga
all those years ago?

8. *Priest Kisen*

I live alone in a simple hut
south-east of the capital,
but people speak of me as one
who fled the sorrows of the world
only to end up on the Hill of Sorrow.

9. *Ono no Komachi*

I have loved in vain
and now my beauty fades
like these cherry blossoms
paling in the long rains of spring
that I gaze upon alone.

10. *Semimaru*

So this is the place!
Crowds,
coming
going
meeting
parting,
those known,
unknown –
the Gate of Meeting Hill.

11. *Ono no Takamura*

Fishing boats upon the sea,
tell whoever asks
that I have sailed away,
out past countless islets
to the vast ocean beyond.

12. Archbishop Henjo

Breezes of Heaven, blow closed
the pathway through the clouds
to keep a little longer
these heavenly dancers
from returning home.

13. Retired Emperor Yozei

Just as the Minano River
surges from the peak
of Mount Tsukuba,
so my love cascades
to make deep pools.

14. *Minamoto no Toru*

My heart's as tangled
as the wild fern patterns
of Michinoku's Shinobu cloth.
Since it is not my fault,
whom should I blame for this?

15. Emperor Koko

For you,
I came out to the fields
to pick the first spring greens.
All the while, on my sleeves
a light snow falling.

16. Ariwara no Yukihira

Though I may leave
for Mount Inaba,
whose peak is covered with pines,
if I hear that you pine for me,
I will come straight home to you.

17. *Ariwara no Narihira*

Such beauty unheard of
even in the age of the raging gods –
the Tatsuta River
tie-dyeing its waters
in autumnal colours.

18. Fujiwara no Toshiyuki

Unlike the waves that approach
the shores of Sumiyoshi Bay,
why do you avoid the eyes of others,
refusing to approach me –
even on the path of dreams?

19. Lady Ise

Are you saying, for even a moment
short as the space
between the nodes on a reed
from Naniwa Inlet,
we should never meet again?

20. *Prince Motoyoshi*

I'm so desperate, it's all the same.
Like the channel markers of Naniwa
whose name means 'self-sacrifice',
let me give up my life
to see you once again.

21. *Priest Sosei*

As you said, 'I'm coming right away,'
I waited for you
through the long autumn night,
but only the moon greeted me
at the cold light of dawn.

22. *Fun'ya no Yasuhide*

In autumn the wind has only to blow
for leaves and grasses to perish.
That must be why the characters
'mountain' and 'wind'
together mean 'gale'.

23. *Oe no Chisato*

Thoughts of a thousand things
fill me with melancholy
as I gaze upon the moon,
but autumn's dejection
comes not to me alone.

24. *Sugawara no Michizane*

On this journey
I have no streamers to offer up.
Instead, dear gods, if it pleases you,
may you take this maple brocade
of Mount Tamuke's colours.

25. *Fujiwara no Sadakata*

If the 'sleep-together vine'
that grows on Meeting Hill
is true to its name,
I will entwine you in my arms,
unknown to anyone.

26. *Fujiwara no Tadahira*

Dear Maples of Mount Ogura,
if you have a heart,
please wait for another visit
so that His Majesty may enjoy
your lovely autumn colours.

27. *Fujiwara no Kanesuke*

When did you first spring into view?
Like the Field of Jars
divided by the River of Springs,
I am split in two – so deeply flows
the river of my love for you.

28. Minamoto no Muneyuki

In my mountain abode
it is winter
that feels loneliest –
both grasses and visitors
dry up.

29. *Oshikochi no Mitsune*

To pluck a stem
I shall have to guess,
for I cannot tell apart
white chrysanthemums
from the first frost.

30. *Mibu no Tadamine*

How cold the face
of the morning moon!
Since we parted
nothing is so miserable
as the approaching dawn.

31. *Sakanoue no Korenori*

Beloved Yoshino –
I was sure you were bathed
in the moonlight of dawn,
but it's a soft falling of snow
that mantles you in white.

32. *Harumichi no Tsuraki*

The weir that the wind
has flung across
the mountain brook
is made of autumn's
richly coloured leaves.

33. *Ki no Tomonori*

Cherry Blossoms,
on this calm, lambent
day of spring,
why do you scatter
with such unquiet hearts?

34. *Fujiwara no Okikaze*

Of those I loved, none are left.
Only the aged pine
of Takasago
has my years, but, alas,
he is not an old friend of mine.

35. Ki no Tsurayuki

As the human heart's so fickle
your feelings may have changed,
but at least in my old home
the plum blossoms bloom as always
with a fragrance of the past.

36. Kiyohara no Fukayabu

On this summer night,
when twilight has so quickly
become the dawn,
where is the moon at rest
among the clouds?

37. Fun'ya no Asayasu

When the wind gusts
over the autumn fields,
white dewdrops
lie strewn about
like scattered pearls.

38. Ukon

Though you have forgotten me,
I do not worry about myself,
but how I fear for you,
as you swore before the gods
of your undying love.

39. *Minamoto no Hitoshi*

I try to conceal my feelings,
but **they** are too much to bear –
like reeds **hi**dden in the **low** bamboo
of this desolate plain.
Why do I love you so?

40. *Taira no Kanemori*

Though I try to keep it secret,
my deep love shows
in the blush on my face.
Others keep asking me –
'*Who* are you thinking of?'

41. *Mibu no Tadami*

I had hoped to keep secret
feelings that had begun to stir
within my heart,
but already rumours are rife
that I am in love with you.

42. *Kiyohara no Motosuke*

Wringing tears from our sleeves,
did we not pledge never to part,
not even if the waves engulfed
the Mount of Forever-Green Pines –
what caused such a change of heart?

43. *Fujiwara no Atsutada*

When I compare my heart
from before we met
to after we made love,
I know I had not yet grasped
the pain of loving you.

44. *Fujiwara no Asatada*

If we had never met,
I would not so much resent
your being cold to me
or how I've come to hate myself
because I love you so.

45. *Fujiwara no Koremasa*

'I feel so sorry for you.'
No one comes to mind
who would say that to me,
so I will surely die alone
of a broken heart.

46. *Sone no Yoshitada*

Crossing the Bay of Yura
the boatman loses the rudder.
The boat is adrift,
not knowing where it goes.
Is the course of love like this?

47. *Priest Egyō*

How lonely this villa
has become, overgrown
with vines and weeds.
No one visits me –
only autumn comes.

48. *Minamoto no Shigeyuki*

Blown by the fierce winds,
I am the waves that crash
upon your impervious rock.
Though my heart shatters,
my love rages yet.

49. *Onakatomi no Yoshinobu*

This troubled heart of mine
is like the watch fire of the guards
of the palace gate –
it fades to embers by day,
but blazes up again each night.

50. Fujiwara no Yoshitaka

I thought I would give up my life
to hold you in my arms,
but after a night together,
I find myself wishing
that I could live for ever.

51. Fujiwara no Sanekata

Because my feelings
are too great to put into words,
my heart blazes like the moxa
of Mount Ibuki,
with a love you cannot know.

52. Fujiwara no Michinobu

Though the sun has risen,
I know I can see you again
when it sets at dusk.
Yet even so, how I hate
this cold light of dawn.

53. *Mother of Michitsuna*

Someone like you
may never know
how long a night can be,
spent pining for a loved one
till it breaks at dawn.

54. *Mother of Honorary Grand Minister*

You promise you'll never forget,
but to the end of time
is too long to ask.
So let me die today –
still loved by you.

55. *Fujiwara no Kinto*

The waterfall
dried up
in the distant past
and makes
not a sound,
but its fame
flows on
and on –
and echoes
still
today.

56. Izumi Shikibu

As I will soon be gone,
let me take one last memory
of this world with me –
may I see you once more,
may I see you now?

57. Murasaki Shikibu

Just like the moon,
you had come and gone
before I knew it.
Were you, too, hiding
among the midnight clouds?

58. *Daini no Sanmi*

Blown down from Mount Arima
through Ina's low bamboo
the wind whispers,
'I swear of my love –
how could I forget you?'

59. Akazome Emon

I should have gone to sleep
but, thinking you would come,
I watched the moon
throughout the night
till it sank before the dawn.

60. *Koshikibu no Naishi*

No letter's come from my mother,
nor have I sought help with this poem,
crossing Mount Oe,
taking the Ikuno Road to her home
beyond the Bridge to Heaven.

61. *Ise no Taifu*

The eightfold cherry blossoms
from Nara's ancient capital
bloom afresh today
in the new capital
of the nine splendid gates.

62. *Sei Shonagon*

Wishing to leave while still night,
you crow like a cock pretending it is dawn.
As I will never meet you again,
may the guards of the Meeting Hill
for ever block your passage through.

63. *Fujiwara no Michimasa*

Rather than hearing it from others,
somehow I want to find a way
to tell you myself,
just one thing –
'Now I must give you up!'

64. *Fujiwara no Sadayori*

As the dawn mist
thins in patches
on the Uji River,
in the shallows appear
glistening stakes of fishing nets.

65. Sagami

Even my sleeves may rot
from bitter tears that never dry,
but worse than that
is the tainting of my name
by this bitter love.

66. *Prelate Gyoson*

Mountain Cherry,
let us console each other.
Of all those I know
no one understands me
the way your blossoms do.

67. Suo no Naishi

I would regret losing my good name
for laying my head upon your arm
offered as a pillow
for a moment as fleeting
as a spring night's dream.

68. Retired Emperor Sanjo

Though against my wishes,
I must live on in this world of pain.
But when I look back
I will surely recall you fondly,
Dear Moon of this darkest night.

69. *Priest Noin*

Blown by storm winds,
Mount Mimuro's
autumn leaves have become
the River Tatsuta's
richly hued brocade.

70. *Priest Ryozen*

With a lonely heart,
I step outside my hut
and look around.
Everywhere's the same –
autumn at dusk.

71. *Minamoto no Tsunenobu*

As evening draws near
in the field before the gate
the autumn wind visits,
rustling through the ears of rice,
then the eaves of my reed hut.

72. *Lady Kii*

I stay well away
from the famed Takashi shore,
where the waves, like you, are treacherous.
I know if I get too close to either,
my sleeves will end up wet.

73. Oe no Masafusa

How lovely the cherry blossoms
blooming high
on the peaks of Takasago.
May the mists in the foothills
not rise to block the view.

74. *Minamoto no Toshiyori*

I pleaded with the Goddess of Mercy
for help with she who was cold to me
but, like the wild winds of Hatsuse,
she became fiercer still.
It is not what I prayed for.

75. *Fujiwara no Mototoshi*

I believed in you with all my heart
but again this autumn passed,
filled with sadness. Your promises –
but vanishing dewdrops
of the mugwort blessing!

76. Fujiwara no Tadamichi

Rowing out on the vast ocean,
when I look all around
I cannot tell apart
white billows in the offing
from the far-off clouds.

77. *Retired Emperor Sutoku*

Like water rushing down
the river rapids,
we may be parted
by a rock, but in the end
we will be one again.

78. *Minamoto no Kanemasa*

Barrier Guard of Suma,
how many nights
have you been wakened
by the lamenting plovers
returning from Awaji?

79. *Fujiwara no Akisuke*

Autumn breezes blow
long trailing clouds.
Through a break,
the moonlight –
so clear, so bright.

80. *Taikenmon-in no Horikawa*

After you left this morning
my raven locks were full of tangles,
and now – not knowing
if you will always be true –
my heart is filled with tangles, too.

81. *Fujiwara no Sanesada*

I look out to where
the little cuckoo called,
but all that is left to see
is the pale moon
in the sky of dawn.

82. *Priest Doin*

I somehow live on,
enduring this harsh love,
yet my tears –
unable to bear their pain –
cannot help but flow.

83. *Fujiwara no Shunzei*

There's no escape in this sad world.
With a melancholy heart
I enter deep in the mountains,
but even here I hear
the plaintive belling of the stag.

84. *Fujiwara no Kiyosuke*

Since I now recall fondly
the painful days of the past,
if I live long, I may look back
on these harsh days, too,
and find them sweet and good.

85. Priest Shun'e

I spent the night in longing
but the day would not break
and even gaps in the shutters
were too cruel
to let in a sliver of light.

86. *Priest Saigyo*

It is not you, Dear Moon,
who bids me grieve
but when I look at your face
I am reminded of my love –
and tears begin to fall.

87. Priest Jakuren

The sudden shower
has not yet dried.
From the leaves of black pines,
wisps of fog rise
in the autumn dusk.

88. *Kokamon-in no Betto*

For the sake of one night
on Naniwa Bay,
short as the nodes
of a root-cut reed,
must I love you with all my heart?

89. *Princess Shokushi*

Should I live longer
I could not bear this secret love.
Jewelled thread of life,
since you must break –
let it be now.

90. *Inpumon-in no Taifu*

How I would like to show you –
the fishermen's sleeves of Ojima
are drenched, but even so
have not lost their colour,
as mine have, bathed in endless tears.

91. *Fujiwara no Ryokei*

The crickets cry
on this frosty night
as I spread my robe for one
on the cold straw mat
where I shall sleep alone.

92. *Lady Sanuki*

My tear-soaked sleeves
are like rocks in the offing.
Even at low tide
you never notice them,
nor can they ever dry.

93. *Minamoto no Sanetomo*

That such moving sights
would never change –
fishermen rowing
their small boats,
pulling them on to shore.

94. *Fujiwara no Masatsune*

A cold mountain wind blows down
on the old capital of Yoshino,
and as the autumn night deepens
I can hear the chilly pounding
of cloth being fulled.

95. *Former High Prelate Jien*

Though I am not good enough,
for the good of the people,
here in these wooded hills,
I'll embrace them in my black robes
of the Buddha's Way.

96. *Fujiwara no Kintsune*

As if lured by the storm
the blossoms are strewn about,
white upon the garden floor,
yet all this whiteness is not snow –
it is me who withers and grows old.

97. Fujiwara no Teika

Pining for you,
who do not come,
I am like the salt-making fires
at dusk on the Bay of Waiting –
burning bitterly in flames of love.

98. *Fujiwara no Ietaka*

A twilight breeze rustles
through the oak leaves
of the little Oak Brook,
but the cleansing rites
tell us it is still summer.

99. *Retired Emperor Gotoba*

Though it is futile to ponder
the ways of the world,
I am lost in desolate musing –
I have loved some and hated others,
even hated the ones I love.

100. *Retired Emperor Juntoku*

Memory ferns sprout in the eaves
of the old forsaken palace.
But however much I yearn for it,
I can never bring back
that glorious reign of old.

Commentary

In the main body of the translation, the poems are provided without any contextual information. As the Introduction explains (p. xvi), Teika is thought to have first selected the poems for decoration on the walls of the country residence of his son's father-in-law, Utsunomiya Rensho. An entry in his diary records that he sent a hundred poems to Rensho for his house and these are thought to be more or less the same as the poems that became the *One Hundred Poems*. At that time Teika excised the headnotes (**kotobagaki**) that originally accompanied the poems in the sources from which they were taken. In other words, Teika presented the poems context-free with no information except the name of the author. The original headnotes describe the circumstances in which the poems were written or merely give the topic (*dai*) on which they were composed; some are short but some give long, detailed accounts – sometimes fictional – describing the background of the composition of the poem.

I have also presented the poems context-free, with no information except the name of the author, so that the reader can encounter them without encumbrances. However, I have included pertinent information from the original headnotes in the Commentary. Although the original headnotes were not always verifiably correct, they do provide interesting details on context that reflect the reception of the poems in the *One Hundred Poets* up to and after Teika's time. I hope the annotations that follow, which also include information on the translation techniques employed, short biographies of the poets and other details, will make the reader's encounter with the text more informed and pleasurable.

As a general point, it should be noted that while the poems were composed at various stages of their authors' lives, the poets are all known by their posthumous names, as in the original collection. Thus although poem 100 was written while the emperor was still reigning, he is known by his posthumous name, Retired Emperor Juntoku. And although poem 95 was composed by Jien when still a young man, he is known by the later title of Former High Prelate Jien. When the names of women poets are not known, they are often referred to as the 'mother' or 'daughter' of someone, such as 'Mother of Michitsuna' (poem 53). Even where the name of a woman poet was known, she might be referred to in this way, such as 'Mother of Honorary Grand Minister' (poem 54), rather than by her actual name, Takashina no Takako.

In the Commentary, full names of historical figures follow the Japanese order of family name followed by forename, with just the forename (rather than the surname) being used otherwise, as in '[Fujiwara no] Teika'. Words and phrases highlighted in bold constitute a reference to the Glossary, where further information may be found on literary terms and conventions and major works of classical Japanese literature that crop up repeatedly in the annotations that follow. The periods of Japanese history referred to are: Nara (710–94); Heian (794–1185); Kamakura (1185–1333); Edo (1603–1868); and Meiji (1868–1912).

The collection opens and closes with poems by emperors, reflecting Teika's emphasis on the connection between the imperial institution and poetry. (See the Introduction, pp. xxv–xxviii, for more on this.) The gentle first poem, about the dew moistening the poet's sleeves in a simple hut, sets the tone for the entire collection. In classical Japanese poetry, wet sleeves are typically associated with tears, usually of despair over an unhappy love relationship. Like the majority of medieval commentators, however, Teika seems to have read the poem as a political allegory in which the wise and caring sovereign, Emperor Tenji, expresses his sympathy for the hardships of his people, symbolized by the ruined state of the hut. This is also the traditional reading of the poem, one that would have resonated most with its original audience, and hence is the version given in the main translation. A stronger, more nuanced reading would be to interpret it as a love poem, in which case it might be rendered:

> In this makeshift hut
> in the autumn field
> gaps in the thatch let dewdrops in,
> but it is not dew alone
> that moistens my sleeves . . .

This reading is advocated, among others, by the eminent *Man'yōshū* scholar Susumu Nakanishi (in *Nakanishi Susumu to aruku Hyakunin isshu no Kyoto* (Kyoto: Kyoto Shinbun, 2007), pp. 7–11). Emperor Tenji is said to have been involved in a heated love triangle with his brother Prince Oama – the future Emperor Tenmu (r. 673–86) – over the love of Princess Nukata, a famed beauty and poet, but no historical evidence supports this.

The image of Tenji as an ideal and benevolent ruler dates from the time of the *Gosenshū* (951), the collection from which Teika took the poem (no. 302), as does the poem's attribution to him, though he was not the original author. The original poem, with slightly different wording appears in the *Man'yōshū* (no. 2178), as 'anonymous'. It is more than likely that the poem underwent modifications as it was passed down from the time of the *Man'yōshū* to the *Gosenshū*.

Emperor Tenji (626–72; r. 661–72) was the thirty-eighth emperor. He vanquished the Soga clan with the help of Nakatomi no Kamatari, on whom he bestowed the family name Fujiwara in 669. He was especially revered by the Fujiwara clan, including Teika (see also the Introduction, p. xxvi). After his death, a succession dispute broke out between his brother Prince Oama and his son Prince Otomo, an event known as the Jinshin disturbance. Oama eventually prevailed and ascended the throne with the name Tenmu.

2

Summer follows autumn in the second poem of the collection. Jito was Tenji's daughter, so by placing her poem after her father's, Teika is stressing the hereditariness of both poetic craft and the imperial house. A famous episode in the *Kojiki* (Record of Ancient Matters; 711–12) describes the sun goddess, Amaterasu, retreating behind a stone door and temporarily plunging the world into darkness. The widely believed setting of the rock door – the supposed rock can still be seen – is Takachiho in present-day Miyazaki Prefecture, but an alternative version of the legend associates it with the Mount Kagu of Yamato Province (present-day Nara Prefecture) in this poem. There is an obvious desire to link the mythic tradition and the empress's earthly benevolence: everything in the poem is whiteness and light, shining with divine auspiciousness.

Commentators have debated whether the white robes mentioned in the poem are meant to be read literally as garments hung out to dry, or as a metaphor for mist or flowers covering the mountain. In medieval times the latter view was prevalent but commentators from the Edo period onwards favoured the former interpretation as it makes the poem more direct and realistic.

Perhaps because of the difficulty of deciphering the writing of the *Man'yōshū*, there are significant differences between the poem as it appears in that collection and as Teika included it both here and in the *Shin-kokinshū* (no. 175). Lines 2 and 4 of the poem in the *Man'yōshū* as we know it today read 'summer seems to have come' and 'robes are hung out to air', making for a direct, observational poem. The later version used by Teika adds an element of indirection ('I hear that . . .'), which is not typical of poetry of the *Man'yōshū* period. The indirection detracts rather from the immediacy of the poem in English, so my translation does not reflect the later emendation, and is closer to the original eighth-century version.

Empress Jito (645–702; r. 686–97), the forty-first ruler of Japan, was the daughter of Emperor Tenji (poem 1). Many of the outstanding poems in the *Man'yōshū* were composed during her reign and it was most probably also during her reign that the idea of compiling the anthology of *waka* that eventually became the *Man'yōshū* was conceived.

3

Poem 3 plays on the great length of a pheasant's tail, the slow passing of a night spent alone, and the belief that the male and female pheasants spent the night in separate valleys. The use of nature to evoke a state of mind is perhaps the single, most conspicuous feature of classical Japanese *waka*. The layout of the poem is a visual representation of the long tail. In five lines, it would read:

> The long tail of the copper pheasant
> trails, drags on and on
> like this long night alone
> in the lonely mountains,
> longing for my love.

Rhetorically, the poem offers a textbook example of the preface (*jokotoba*), in which the initial part of the poem (the preface), describing the landscape, and the second part, describing the feelings of the poet, are connected by a **pivot word** (the adjective 'long', *naganagashi*) that links the first part of the poem – 'the *long long* tail of the copper pheasant' – with the latter part: '*long long* nights spent alone'.

In the original, the repetition of the sounds *na* and *o* makes the night seem even longer, and the translation attempts to create a similar effect by employing assonance and alliteration (e.g. 'long', 'alone', 'lonely', 'love' and 'longing'). The feelings of longing for the beloved in the last four lines are only implied in the original, which limits itself to saying 'alone I sleep'.

Although Teika and his contemporaries believed the poem to be by Hitomaro, the authorship is in fact unknown. A variant of the poem in the *Man'yōshū* (no. 2812) is given as 'anonymous', with a note stating that in other works it is attributed to Hitomaro. Given Hitomaro's unrivalled fame, it is quite possible that this poem originally opened the *One Hundred Poets*, and that it came to be the third poem only when Teika decided to place verses by an emperor and an empress at the beginning of the collection.

Kakinomoto no Hitomaro (*fl.* late seventh century) is universally considered one of the greatest Japanese poets of all time. The poems that can be safely attributed to him all appear in the *Man'yōshū*. They total eighty-eight poems, eighteen *chōka* and seventy *tanka*, but many more have been attributed to him in later collections, more or less dubiously. He is one of the four great poets of the *Man'yōshū* period; the others are Akahito (poem 4), Yakamochi (poem 6) and Yamanoue no Okura (660?–733?).

Hitomaro's greatness was already recognized by Tsurayuki (poem 35), who hails him as the 'sage of poetry' (*uta no hijiri*) in the *Kokinshū* preface. His fame grew only in later centuries when he came to be regarded as the god of Japanese poetry (*uta no kami*), a reputation that is well deserved. Whereas much later poetry tends to be purely elegant and decorative, Hitomaro's poems often fuse refinement of expression with majesty and power. He coined many of the images and expressions that later become stock phrases in poetry. Scholars believe that many of the 'pillow words' (*makura kotoba*) used in *waka* were created by him.

4

This is an early example of one of many poems, especially in classical Japanese literature, that feature Mount Fuji. The snow-covered top and gently sloping sides of the mountain have inspired writers and artists for centuries, famously Hokusai (1760–1849) in his *Thirty-Six Views of Mount Fuji* (*c.*1830–32), one of which, 'The Shore of Tago Bay, Ejiri at Tokaido', is based on this very poem. The poem is also an early example of 'landscape poetry' (*jokeika*). The majestic silhouette of Mount Fuji, covered in white snow and towering over the dazzling blueness of Tago Bay (both famous poetic locations – see *utamakura*), is evoked in all its breathtaking beauty. Fuji is depicted mostly as a female mountain in Japanese literature, hence the female attribution, though it can be referred to as male or, on rare occasions, both male and female.

Teika took the poem from the *Shin-kokinshū* (no. 675); an earlier version of the poem in the *Man'yōshū* (no. 321) has 'has fallen' (*furikeru*) in the last line instead of 'still falling' (*furitsutsu*). This rather minor difference has been the subject of much debate. Medieval commentators seem to have preferred 'continues to fall', and the ethereal beauty it conveys, to the original wording; later critics held the opposite view, arguing that replacing *furikeru* with *furitsutsu* greatly diminished the value of the poem by making it less immediate and direct.

Yamabe no Akahito (*fl.* first half of eighth century) was a Nara-period courtier and bureaucrat who served under Emperor Shomu (r. 724–49). Akahito is ranked as one of the four great poets of the *Man'yōshū* period (see commentary to poem 3). He has thirteen *chōka* and thirty-seven *tanka* in the *Man'yōshū*, and is listed by Kinto (poem 55) among his **Thirty-Six Poetic Geniuses**.

5

Seasonal poems of the *Kokinshū* period (early tenth century) often combine two or more images from nature, a poetic device known in Japanese as *kumiawase*. This poem presents one of the classic autumnal combinations: maple leaves (*momiji*) and deer (*shika*). Other common combinations are cherry blossoms and the bush warbler for spring, and orange blossom and the cuckoo for summer.

The deer's plaintive cry has featured in Japanese poetry since earliest times, usually as a metaphor for longing for a distant lover. Classical Japanese poetry often avoids use of the subject marker and this poem is a good example. Two different readings are possible depending on whether one takes the deer or the poet as the subject of 'making a path through the fallen leaves' (see the Note on the Translation, p. xliii).

The poem is traditionally attributed to the legendary poet Sarumaru, about whom very little is known except that he is mentioned in various Heian texts. Teika also attributes the poem to Sarumaru, although he would have known that it was in fact composed for a poetry contest at the house of Prince Koresada (*c.*893), an important early competition at which many of the conventions of what is today known as the '*Kokinshū* style' were first established. The poem appears in the *Kokinshū* (no. 215) as 'anonymous' and the author remains unknown.

Sarumaru Taifu (*fl.* mid eighth century, according to tradition, though there are no records to prove that he was an actual historical figure), aka Sarumaru Dayu, is listed by Kinto (poem 55) among his **Thirty-Six Poetic Geniuses**. A later collection entitled *Sarumaru Dayū* exists, but the attribution of the poems in it to him is doubtful.

6

Poem 6 is based on the Tanabata legend, a prominent poetic topic (*dai*) since early times. Originating in China, the legend has long been popular in Japan and many poems have been written on it from the *Man'yōshū* onwards. According to the legend, the Weaving Maid, Orihime (the star Vega), can meet her lover, the Herd Boy, Hikoboshi (the star Altair), only once a year, on the seventh day of the seventh month – the day on which the festival associated with the legend is also held – when a flock of magpies form a bridge over the Milky Way. The Tanabata festival is today celebrated every year on 7 July at the end of the rainy season. In the **lunisolar calendar**, in use in ancient times, however, it fell in mid August, in full summer.

Opinions differ, however, as to whether the poem is to be interpreted literally, as a rendering of the Tanabata legend, or allegorically, as a beautiful description of palace life making use of elements of the legend. Commentators from the Edo-period scholar Kamo no Mabuchi (1696–1769) onwards have argued that the bridge of magpie wings is probably a picturesque way to refer to bridges or stairs within the imperial compound, especially those that lovers would cross at night on their way to and from their secret liaisons. Secrecy was of the utmost importance in the ritual of courtly love, and being seen on a nightly wander by the frost-covered bridge mentioned in the poem would have been considered highly elegant. The bridge of magpie wings itself (intended for those who lived above the clouds) could designate the imperial palace as much as the legend. In my translation, both readings of the poem are possible and the reader may choose one or the other or enjoy both. The line 'the lovers will cross' is not in the original.

Otomo no Yakamochi (718?–785) is one of the four great poets of the *Man'yōshū* period (see commentary to poem 3), with the largest number of poems in the *Man'yōshū*, 479 in total (forty-six *chōka*, 431 *tanka*, one *sedōka* and one poem in Chinese (see *kanshi*)). The last four parts of the *Man'yōshū* read almost like a poetic diary, giving rise to the theory that Yakamochi must be the compiler of the final version of the anthology.

7

Poem 7 is the first of many in the collection that features the moon (poems 21, 23, 30, 31, 36 and 57 are some other examples). Here the moon reminds the poet of his distant home in the city of Nara. The poem appears in the *Kokinshū* (no. 406) with an accompanying headnote (*kotobagaki*) stating that it was composed by Abe no Nakamaro when he was in China. Nakamaro went to China in 717 as part of an official mission. He attempted to travel back to Japan in 753 after being granted permission by the Chinese emperor, but his ship was wrecked on the coast of Vietnam and he was forced to return to China, where he died without ever making it back home.

Kasuga Shrine, by Mount Mikasa in the city of present-day Nara, was where courtiers went to pray for a safe return before leaving for China, and Nakamaro probably had paid his respects there before leaving Japan. The shrine and the mountain are both famous poetic locations (see *utamakura*). Nakamaro is said to have composed this poem on the very night of his farewell party before attempting to return to Japan. For centuries the poem has epitomized the traveller's nostalgia for home.

Abe no Nakamaro (701–770) was a courtier and poet. During his time in China he befriended poets Li Bai (701–62) and Wang Wei (701–61) and was noticed by Emperor Xuanzong of Tang (r. 712–56), who inducted him into his entourage. At the age of thirty-seven, he was made Director of Protections and put in control of the Three Offices (Arms, Arsenal and Palace Guards). After the shipwreck in 753, he was forced to return to Chang'an in China, where he stayed until he died.

8

The theme of poem 8 is the gossip that has followed the poet's deci-
sion to leave the capital for a life of quiet retreat. Uji, south-east of
Kyoto, is a place name (*utamakura*) that was frequently used in
poetry, whether in the form of the mountain, as here, or the river (see
poem 64). In the Japanese, Uji can be read as *ushi* (sad, sorrowful) and
hence was often used as a pun. In early *kana* orthography there were
no vocalization markers, so when words were written down, no dif-
ference was made between voiced and unvoiced consonants (*shi* and
ji, *ha* and *ba*, etc.). Thus Uji and *ushi* can be read in the same way.

Some commentators – including Teika himself – believed that
there was another pun between the emphatic particle *shika* and *shika*
meaning 'deer', known for its plaintive cry, but that view is not
generally held today, and is not reflected in the translation. Lexical
acrobatics of this kind were particularly popular in the author's time,
which literary historians call the period of the **Six Poetic Geniuses**
(*Rokkasen jidai, c.* mid ninth century). In the translation, I have trans-
lated Uji as 'Hill of Sorrow' to convey the flavour of the original pun.

Uji is also well known as the setting of the last ten chapters of *The
Tale of Genji*, which, in keeping with the name of the location, are
characterized by a particularly gloomy tone.

Priest Kisen (*fl.* mid ninth century). Next to nothing is known about
him except what can be deduced from this one poem – that he was a
Buddhist monk and lived in the Uji area. In the headnote (*kotoba-
gaki*) to the poem in the *Kokinshū* (no. 983), Kisen's diction is said to
be vague, and his poems are said to lack a clear structure, but as no
other by him survives, it is impossible to tell if this criticism is justi-
fied. The present poem displays none of these flaws. Another work he
is said to have written, the *Kisen shiki* (Kisen's Rules of Composition),
is almost certainly apocryphal.

9

Poem 9 is the most rhetorically brilliant and sophisticated in the col-
lection, and a full description of the techniques can be found in the
Introduction (p. xxix) and Note on the Translation (pp. xliii–xlv). The

main theme is the evanescence of all things (*mujōkan*), a prominent concept in Japanese literature that is expressed here with extraordinary verbal artistry.

The poem contains a **pivot word**, *itazurani* (in vain), linking the first part, 'the flowers lose their colour *in vain*', with the second, '*in vain* I have passed through this world'. There are also two puns (**kakekotoba**): *furu* (both 'to rain' and 'to pass') and *nagame* ('to gaze at' and 'long rains'). Through punning, two different but interconnected layers of meaning are created: an image of endless rains slowly washing away the colour of the flowers; and a picture of a woman past her prime who just sits in idle longing.

While the loss of youthful beauty is lamented universally, it was especially feared in Heian-period Japan. A woman's fortune at the imperial court depended upon her appearance, hence great importance was attached to it. The poem can be read either as the cry of an ageing lady whose days of glory at court have passed or as the lament of a woman who knows that her prime is passing as her lover now neglects her. I have chosen to follow this latter interpretation, although the other is equally acceptable and perhaps more common. (See the Introduction, p. xxix, for more on this.)

Ono no Komachi (*fl.* mid ninth century) was probably a lady-in-waiting during the reigns of emperors Ninmyo (r. 833–50) and Montoku (r. 850–58). She is said to have been a great beauty who treated her lovers cruelly, though this is almost certainly a later legend. Only her twenty-one poems in the **Kokinshū** and **Gosenshū** are considered authentic, but a great many more are attributed to her in later sources. The *Komachi-shū* (Collected Poems of Komachi), compiled long after her death, includes poems by others too. She appears in seven extant **Noh** plays, five of them in the regular repertory, and even a new Noh play, *Fumigara* (The Love Letters), by Tsumura Kimiko (1902–74), which shows the enduring interest in her. She is in Kinto's list of **Thirty-Six Poetic Geniuses**, as well as the **Thirty-Six Women Poetic Geniuses**, and is the only woman poet in Tsurayuki's **Six Poetic Geniuses**. So many details about Komachi's life have been fabricated that it is impossible to separate the real person from the literary creation. But what is in no doubt is the majestic power of her best poems and their exquisite depiction of the frailty of the human condition.

10

Poem 10 is unique in the collection in the way in which the rhythm of its lines creates a marvellous sense of movement. The theme is once again the fragility of life, this time expressed through the evanescence of life's encounters, including those of love.

The Osaka Barrier (translated here as 'the Gate of Meeting Hill'), situated on the edge of Lake Biwa, near Kyoto, marked the border between the ancient provinces of Yamashiro and Omi, dividing the eastern and western parts of Japan. In poetry it was used to signify a meeting place between travellers and, by extension, lovers, because the *au* in Ausaka, the archaic spelling of Osaka, puns with *au*, to meet, especially in the context of a romantic encounter, and hence the name meant something like 'meeting hill'. (See also **utamakura** and poems 25 and 62.)

Pondering on binaries, as the poet does here, is common enough in ninth-century poetry; poem 2 in the **Kokinshū** is another example:

> Is life real
> or but a dream?
> I do not know
> for one moment it's here –
> but gone the next.

> *(Yo no naka wa / yume ka utsutsu ka / utsutsu tomo /*
> *yume tomo shirazu / arite nakereba)*

A more literal translation of *wakarete wa* in line 3 of poem 10 would read 'here they part ways'. I have translated the poem using single-word lines to convey some of the energy and sense of movement of the original poem. A more conventional rendering would be:

> So this is the place!
> Crowds coming, going,
> here they part ways,
> those known, unknown –
> the Gate of Meeting Hill.

Semimaru (*fl.* early tenth century). Little is known about him. He is said to have lived as a hermit by the Osaka Barrier. A legend grew around him that he was a son of Emperor Daigo (r. 897–930), banished because of his blindness (seen as a retribution for sins in a past life), and he is believed to have been a virtuoso *biwa* lutenist. Four poems are attributed to him in the imperial *waka* anthologies; he is also the subject of Zeami's great **Noh** play *Semimaru*.

II

This is another poem on the theme of exile (see also poem 7). Takamura was exiled to the Oki Islands for refusing to join the mission to China in 838 over divergences with the ambassador, Fujiwara no Tsunenaga. He was pardoned in 840, however, and resumed his position at court. According to the headnote (*kotobagaki*) in the *Kokinshū*, Takamura wrote the poem before boarding the boat that would take him to the islands and had it sent back to someone in the capital to convey the sadness he felt upon departing.

An alternative way of interpreting the poem is as a love poem addressed to a lady in the capital:

> Boats of the fisherman,
> tell her, please,
> I'm being rowed away to exile
> through the myriad islets
> to the great ocean beyond.

Here the poet is being 'rowed away to exile', as a nobleman would not be expected to row himself. While the word 'exile' does not appear in the original, the 'myriad islets' would indicate to readers of the time that the poet had been sent away and was heading to one of the islands in the Oki archipelago to which people were exiled (see also commentary to poem 100 and *utamakura*). In the main translation, the English idiom 'sailed away' is used instead to convey the poet's sense of disappearing for a long time, possibly for ever; in reality, he was of course pardoned and able to return quite soon.

Teika does not seem to have rated this poem particularly highly (of the various poetry selections that he compiled, the only other collection that he included it in was his *Hachidaishō* (Selection from the First Eight *Waka* Anthologies; 1215–16); his decision to include it here was probably due to non-literary factors (such as the similarities with Emperor Gotoba's experience; see commentary to poem 99).

Ono no Takamura (802–52) was a statesman and literary figure from a distinguished family of scholars. He excelled in both Chinese- and Japanese-language genres. Though a collection of his works in Chinese has been lost, some of his poems and prose works still exist, appearing in collections of Chinese texts such as the *Keikokushū* (Collection to Rule the Realm; 827), the *Wakan rōeishū* (Collection of Chinese and Japanese Poems to Sing; *c.*1018?) and *Honchō monzui* (Literary Selection of Our Realm; mid eleventh century). Six of his *waka* poems are included in the *Kokinshū*.

12

According to the headnote (*kotobagaki*) to the poem as it appears in the *Kokinshū* (no. 872), this poem was composed 'on seeing the Gosechi dancers'. The Gosechi dance was performed at court by young maidens of the nobility. In the year that a new emperor ascended the throne it was performed three times: at the Ninamesai Festival, which celebrated the harvest; at the Daijosai Festival, traditionally held during the eleventh month of the **lunisolar calendar**; and at the Toyoakari no Sechie Festival held the following day.

According to legend, the dance originated in the time of Emperor Tenmu (r. 673–86). The young emperor was playing the *koto* at the Katte Shrine in Yoshino when heavenly dancers appeared above him in the sky. By likening real-life dancers to their heavenly counterparts, the poet equates the earthly realm of the emperor (Ninmyo in this instance) with the immortal abode of the gods. Vivid descriptions of the Gosechi Festival can be found in *The Tale of Genji*. The late-medieval commentary on the *One Hundred Poets*, *Oeishō* (Commentary Written in the Thirteenth Year of Oei; 1406), says of this poem: 'Both the wording and the sentiment are without equal. Some say that it is because such poems are rare in Henjo's oeuvre that this particular one appealed to Teika.'

Archbishop Henjo (816–90), lay name Yoshimine no Munesada, was one of the foremost poets of the ninth century. He served under Emperor Ninmyo (833–50) as Captain of the Imperial Guard and entered religion in 849 after the emperor's sudden demise. *The Tales of Yamato* includes stories of his various loves and religious conversion. Henjo left a private collection of poems. In the *Kokinshū* headnote to the poem here, his work is described as being formally accomplished but lacking in 'truth' (*makoto*). His son Sosei (poem 21) was also a distinguished poet.

13

Poem 13, one of the most beautiful and universal in the collection, appears in the 'Love' section of the *Gosenshū* (no. 777) with the headnote (*kotobagaki*) 'Sent to the Princess of the Fishing Pavilion'. The princess was Suishi (or Yasuko; d. 925), a daughter of Emperor Koko (poem 15). Mount Tsukuba, in the then remote province of Hitachi (modern Ibaraki), was the site of ancient agricultural rituals known as *utagaki* or *kagai*, which involved sexual intercourse between young men and women of marriageable age. The mountain itself has two summits, the Woman's Peak and the Man's Peak, and from ancient times it was associated with love.

Medieval commentators make much of the fact that the poet is an emperor: when an emperor's mind is filled with longing for love, the entire country rejoices; when it is afflicted by problems, the whole country suffers. Associated with imperial benevolence, as it is here, Mount Tsukuba is a famous site (see *utamakura*) referred to in a number of headnotes to poems in the *Kokinshū*.

The first three lines of the poem in the original Japanese, up to and including *Minanogawa*, form a 'preface' (*jokotoba*) to *fuchi* (deep pools), thus introducing a geographical setting (River Minano flowing from Mount Tsukuba) that serves as a metaphor for the idea expressed in the second part of the poem (the depth of the poet's love). Profound love is here compared to the Minano River, which, on falling from Mount Tsukuba, forms deep pools.

Retired Emperor Yozei (868–949; r. 876–84), fifty-seventh emperor and eldest son of Emperor Seiwa (r. 858–76), is remembered more for his extravagance and excess (which included murdering a courtier with his own hands) than for his wisdom as a ruler. In 884, he was eventually forced to abdicate by his uncle, the regent Mototsune, in favour of Emperor Koko. After his retirement he hosted poetry contests and seems to have taken a keen interest in **waka**, though only this one poem was included in the imperial anthologies. His son Prince Motoyoshi (poem 20) was a famous poet and lover.

14

As is often the case in classical Japanese poetry, nature provides a repertoire of images for expressing deep emotion. Here the tangled fern pattern (*shinobu mojizuri*) that symbolizes the poet's inner turmoil was obtained by impressing (*zuri*; literally 'rubbing') a pattern on to fabric using the sap of the hare's foot fern (*shinobu-gusa*). The word *shinobu* (to love secretly) is also the name of an area in north-eastern Japan – a famous poetic location (see **utamakura**). *Michinoku* (literally, 'deep on the road'), the old name for the eastern part of present-day Tohoku, implies a place that is far away and remote. Thus line 3 could also be translated as 'Shinobu cloth of the far-off north'. *Michinoku no / shinobu mojizuri* forms a preface (**jokotoba**) for *midare*, which means 'dishevelled' or 'confused' in reference to the poet's feelings.

Although the original context of the poem is unknown, the poem itself is famous for being quoted in Episode 1 of *The Tales of Ise*, where it serves as the model for a poem by the hero, Ariwara no Narihira (see also poem 17):

> Lavender shoots
> on the Plain of Kasuga,
> like the riotous patterns
> of this purple robe –
> what tangled feelings you arouse!

The hero has just caught a glimpse of two beautiful sisters living in straitened circumstances and borrows the imagery of Toru's poem to express his confused delight at such a sight. His spontaneous composition, based on a famous poem from the past, displays both his talent as a poet and a refinement that made him the ideal lover of the Heian period.

Minamoto no Toru (822–95), the son of Emperor Saga (r. 809–23), was a great aesthete. He was named Kawara Minister of the Left after his residence in the capital to the east of the Sixth Avenue, near the river beach, or *kawara*. In addition to the Kawara mansion, which is the focal point of Episode 81 in *The Tales of Ise*, he was also the owner of a villa at Uji (the site upon which the famous Byodoin Temple was built). Among his achievements was the construction of a magnificent garden in which he recreated miniature versions of various famous locations. The author of two poems each in the *Kokinshū* and *Gosenshū*, he is also the protagonist of a famous **Noh** play, *Tōru*, attributed to Zeami.

15

The theme of this poem is the annual picking of young shoots (*wakana-tsumi*), which took place every year as part of the celebrations for the Day of the Rat (*ne no hi*). The date fell early in the first month (New Year in the **lunisolar calendar** and mid February in the Gregorian calendar). The 'greens' referred to in the poem were the so-called 'seven herbs' (*nanakusa*), namely, *seri* (water dropwort), *nazuna* (shepherd's purse), *gogyō* (cudweed), *hakobera* (chickweed), *hotoke-no-za* (nipplewort), *suzuna* (modern name, *kabu*; Japanese turnip) and *suzushiro* (modern name, *daikon*; radish). Young shoots were thought to symbolize long life and ward off evil, so they were presented as gifts. In the *Man'yōshū* period, the picking would have been done by a woman and the recipient of the gift would have been a man, but in Heian times men also presented such gifts. Here the author is a man. The Festival of the Seven Herbs (*nanakusa no sekku*) is still celebrated today on 7 January. Customs include eating rice porridge flavoured with the aforementioned seven plants. Whereas the young shoots symbolize spring, the falling snow means it is still winter, making this a perfect early-spring poem.

Emperor Koko (830–87: r. 884–7), the fifty-eighth emperor, was the third son of Emperor Ninmyo (r. 833–50) and a protégé of regent Fujiwara no Mototsune. He was enthroned at the age of fifty-four in succession to the mentally unstable Yozei (poem 13). In contemporary sources, he is referred to as the Emperor of the Ninna Era. Fourteen poems by him appear in the imperial *waka* anthologies and he has his own collection, the *Ninna gyoshū*.

16

This poem displays mastery of the technique of literary punning (*kakekotoba*), providing one of the very few examples of a pun that works in both Japanese and English. The word *matsu* shares the same two meanings in Japanese and in English ('pine tree' and 'to pine for someone') and translators since William N. Porter (1849–1929) have consistently exploited this. Another pun used to great effect is based on the place name Inaba, which also means 'if I leave'. Mount Inaba (*Inaba no yama*) also constitutes a famous 'poem pillow' (*utamakura*).

The author of the poem, Yukihira, was appointed Governor of Inaba (present-day Tottori Prefecture) in 855, and may have composed this as a farewell poem for a lover or a friend, though no one knows for certain. It is included in the *Kokinshū* (no. 365) in the category 'Parting'.

Ariwara no Yukihira (818–93) was a grandson of Emperor Heizei (r. 806–9) and the eldest brother of Narihira (poem 17). Known as a man of superior taste, he rose fairly high in the court hierarchy, reaching the third rank and the office of Middle Counsellor (*chūnagon*). The **Noh** play *Matsukaze* (Wind in the Pines), one of the most highly regarded in the entire Noh repertoire, tells of the love between Yukihira and two sisters in what was then the remote seaside location of Suma, and of the sisters' waiting for his return after his departure.

17

Aptly placed after Yukihira's poem, poem 17 is by his more famous younger brother, Narihira, indicating how, in addition to many pairs of poems by fathers and sons/daughters, the *One Hundred Poets* also features a pair of siblings, signifying the importance of familial ties in the *waka* tradition and in Teika's understanding of it.

The poem can be read in two different ways depending on how the fifth line is interpreted. Teika seems to have read it as *mizu kuguru to wa* (water streams below [the maple leaves]), whereas the common interpretation in Narihira's time was in all probability *mizu kukuru to wa* ([the maple leaves] dye the water). (See also the Introduction, p. xx.)

Such differing interpretations were possible because of polysemy, which arose partially from the way in which the ancient *kana* syllabary was written: there was no vocalization mark, so consonants could be read as either voiced or voiceless. (In this case, the second syllable in *kukuru* could be read either as 'ku' or 'gu', giving rise to the two meanings mentioned above: *kuguru* and *kukuru*, 'streams below' and 'dye'). In translation, Teika's version of the poem reads:

> Such beauty unheard of,
> even in the age of the raging gods –
> on the River Tatsuta,
> a carpet of autumn reds,
> water streaming below.

Tatsuta in the ancient Yamato Province originally had a range of different poetic associations (see also **utamakura** and poem 69), but from the Heian period onwards it was used almost exclusively in conjunction with maple leaves. The poem is full of the vigour and slightly iconoclastic charm that one finds in much of Narihira's best verse. The claim that never before has such a spectacle been seen seems to ask the reader to forget the accepted wisdom about the famous location and look at it with fresh eyes.

According to the headnote (**kotobagaki**) that precedes it in the *Kokinshū* (no. 294), the poem was composed as a screen poem (*byōbu-uta*) for the consort of Emperor Seiwa (r. 858–76), Fujiwara no Takaiko (842–910). Such poems were written on paper squares and pasted next to the paintings on folding partition screens. Because they were based on the scene painted on the screen they tend to be strongly visual, and this poem is no exception. (See the Introduction, p. xxv, for more on this.)

This particular poem praises the empress's glory for giving birth to a crown prince, the future Emperor Yozei (poem 13). In Japanese mythology, the gods are the ancestors of the imperial house, so by invoking the age of the gods Narihira is actually paying tribute to the empress. Narihira was part of a circle at Takaiko's palace that included other notable poets, including Priest Sosei (poem 21). The poem also includes a **makura kotoba** (pillow word), *chihayaburu* (raging), which is paired with *kami* (gods) to convey a sense of their awe-inspiring power and, by extension, the unparalleled beauty of the maples.

Poem 17 appears in *The Tales of Ise* (Episode 106) but within the context of a prose tale. In this version, the poem is composed by the hero along the banks of the Tatsuta River where he is out rambling with some princes. Such reworking of famous poems was common practice at the time.

Ariwara no Narihira (825–80) was one of the greatest poets of the early Heian period and a legendary lover. The son of Prince Abo, he was the grandson of Emperor Heizei (r. 806–9) on his father's side and of Kanmu (r. 781–806) on his mother's. His amorous exploits are recorded (alongside some fictional ones) in the *The Tales of Ise*, of which he is believed to be the partial author. Eighty-seven of his poems appear in the imperial *waka* anthologies. He is listed as one of Tsurayuki's **Six Poetic Geniuses** and again in Kinto's **Thirty-Six Poetic Geniuses**.

18

This wonderfully elliptic poem perfectly embodies the witty, sophisticated compositional style of the *Kokinshū* period. The word *yoru* in the Japanese puns on 'to approach' and 'night', indicating that the lovers could only meet by night. I have tried to create a similar effect in the translation by using 'approach' in contrasting ways: the movement of the waves towards the shore and the refusal of the poet's lover to come to him. Although composed by a man, the poem is written from the perspective of a woman longing for her lover (see *matsu onna*). I have left out 'night' from the translation because it is obvious from the reference to the 'path of dreams'.

The first three lines are a preface (*jokotoba*) that is connected to the rest by the **pivot word** *yoru*. The first half of the poem can be read 'the waves approach the shores of Sumiyoshi Bay *even by night*', and the latter part as '*even by night* you refuse to visit me'. Sumiyoshi Bay is also a well-known poetic location (see *utamakura*).

The path of dreams was the path that lovers travelled by night in their dreams to visit their beloved. In this poem it appears that the lover's fear of being seen is so great that he does not dare to visit his beloved even in his dreams. The image of the *yume no kayoiji* (the path of dreams) was often employed in poetry of the Heian period. Its first appearance was as a variation of the word *yumeji* in two beautiful poems by Ono no Komachi in the *Kokinshū* (nos. 657 and 658).

The poem was composed at a famous poetry contest at the house of the Kampyo Empress, an important early contest held in 892, possibly to gather poems for what eventually became the *Kokinshū*.

Fujiwara no Toshiyuki (d. 901). In addition to his poetic talents, he was also a celebrated calligrapher who served under four different emperors. In 897 he became Captain of the Imperial Guard of the Right. Toshiyuki has twenty-nine poems in the imperial *waka* anthologies and a private collection. He is one of Kinto's **Thirty-Six Poetic Geniuses**.

19

This poem employs one of the most famous 'poem pillows' or *utamakura*, the Naniwa Inlet (see also poems 20 and 88). Demarking the area of the Yodo River estuary near present-day Osaka, it was well known for the reeds (*ashi*) referred to in the poem and was used in love poetry to signify intense feelings of love (see commentary to poem 20). It also appears in the *Kokinshū* preface in one of the most famous poems in classical Japanese literature:

> At Naniwa Bay,
> blossoms bloom.
> Blossoms that slept
> through winter,
> now bloom in spring.

Like the previous poem, poem 19 deals with the difficulty of meeting a lover. From a rhetorical perspective, it provides an excellent example of how a **pivot phrase** functions, creating two entirely different sets of readings. The phrase *fushi mo ma* (a very short space/time) indicates both the tiny distance between the nodes on a reed and the brevity of a furtive encounter. In the Japanese, it acts as a pivot between 'should we never meet again for even the *shortest time*' and '*short as the space* between the nodes on a reed', emphasizing the connection between the natural imagery (the reeds of the Naniwa Inlet) and the experience of the unhappy lover who cannot see her beloved. The word *yo* acts as a pun (**kakekotoba**), meaning both 'node' and 'this world', and is an associative word (**engo**) for *ashi* (reed). The whole of line 4 in the original, *awade kono yo o* (not meet in this world), is translated here as 'never meet again'.

Prior to Teika, the poem seems not to have been considered one of Ise's finest (it is not among the ten poems by Ise that Fujiwara no Kinto included in his anthology *Sanjūrokuninshū*), but Teika must have rated it highly because in addition to including it here he also placed it in his selection of the finest **waka** poems, the *Kindai shūka* (Superior Poems of Our Time; 1209).

Lady Ise (*c.*875–*c.*938) was the foremost female poet of the early tenth century. She was a lady-in-waiting to Onshi, consort to Emperor Uda (r. 887–97), and after the death of her mistress she herself became one of Uda's wives and bore him a child. Her daughter Nakatsukasa was also a distinguished poet, but for some reason Teika did not include her in the *One Hundred Poets*. Twenty-two of her poems appear in the *Kokinshū* and seventy-two in the *Gosenshū*.

20

Like the previous two poems, this one is also about overcoming difficulties in love, with a vow to persevere, whatever obstacles might lie in the way: 'Despite the grief I feel, I intend to continue to see you, should it cost me my life.' The headnote (**kotobagaki**) that precedes this poem in the *Gosenshū* (no. 961) provides some context: 'Sent to the Kyogoku consort, after their affair had caused a ruckus.' The Kyogoku consort was Fujiwara no Hoshi, a daughter of the powerful Fujiwara minister Tokihira (871–909). She became one of Emperor Uda's consorts and bore him three sons. The author of the poem, Motoyoshi, was a famous lover and it seems that his courting of Hoshi, a future empress, must have created a scandal.

Rhetorically, the poem features a pun (**kakekotoba**) on *miotsukushi* (channel markers) and *mi o tsukusu*, rendered *mi-o-tsukushite* in the original Japanese (to give up everything, including one's life, for the sake of something). It was one that was commonly used in Heian poetry, often in association with the Naniwa Inlet, the entryway to the capital from the sea (see **utamakura**). Channel markers marked the safe course of navigation for boats sailing to and from the Heian capital. There may also be a second pun in the *na* in Naniwa, meaning 'name' or 'reputation', in which case, *mi-o-tsukushite* might refer to sacrificing not just one's life but one's reputation.

Prince Motoyoshi (890–943), son of Emperor Yozei (poem 13), was known in his time as a great gallant. He figures in several episodes of *The Tales of Yamato*. Twenty of his poems appear in the imperial *waka* anthologies and his poems were collected in the *Motoyoshi shinnō-shū*.

21

Male Heian courtiers often assumed a female persona when composing poems. In this poem, the poet adopts the persona of a woman waiting for her lover. The poem is an example of the subgenre known as the 'waiting woman' (*matsu onna*). Because of social conventions, aristocratic women had to wait for their lovers to visit, often in vain. As the conceit became a literary convention, poems in this style were composed regardless of whether the poet had actually experienced such romantic misadventures.

Lines 3 and 4, 'through the long autumn night, / but only the moon greeted me' (*nagatsuki no / ariake no tsuki o*), are usually thought to refer to a single night – the sense conveyed by this translation – but Teika interpreted them as entire months spent waiting in vain for a visit, giving the poem a more tale-like atmosphere in keeping with the taste of the Heian court.

Priest Sosei (*fl.* late ninth/early tenth century), lay name Yoshimine no Harutoshi, was the son of Yoshimine no Munesada (Archbishop Henjo, poem 12) and is said to have entered religion at the urging of his father. A renowned poet and calligrapher, he is one of Kintō's **Thirty-Six Poetic Geniuses**. He was a favourite of Emperor Uda (r. 887–97) and thirty-six of his poems appear in the *Kokinshū*, making him the fourth best-represented poet in that anthology. His poems were collected in the *Sosei hōshi-shū*.

22

This is one of the very few poems that is based mostly on wordplay. The poem revolves around the idea that the Chinese ideograph for the word 'storm' (*arashi*: 嵐) is made by placing the character for 'mountain' (*yama*: 山) on top of the character for 'wind' (*kaze*: 風). There is also wit in the way *arashi* evokes the word *arasu* (to wreck or destroy). Such clever wordplay was highly popular in mid-Heian times. It was said not to be the taste of Teika and his contemporaries, who required a more serious emotional basis for poetry. Yet it is clear that Teika thought well of this poem because, quite apart from the ingenious wordplay, it is very lyrical, beautifully evoking the harsh autumnal landscape. Indeed, he included it in *Eiga no taigai* (A Rough Guide to Writing Poetry), as an example of a good poem.

Fun'ya no Yasuhide (*fl.* second half of the ninth century), aka Bun'ya no Yasuhide. After serving as a provincial official, he was appointed Second Director of the Imperial Wardrobe in 879, perhaps in recognition of his poetic talent rather than any specific administrative competence. He is mentioned in both the Chinese and Japanese prefaces in the **Kokinshū**. He has six poems in the imperial *waka* anthologies, five of them in the *Kokinshū*. He is one of Tsurayuki's **Six Poetic Geniuses**.

23

This beautiful poem is thought to be an adaptation of a couplet by the Chinese Tang poet Bai Juyi (772–846):

> In Swallow Tower on a seventh-month night,
> autumn comes to find you growing old alone.

The subject of Bai Juyi's poem is Guan Panpan, a singing girl who was the favourite of Minister Zhang Yin and who remained loyal to him after his death by continuing to live alone in a building within his residence called Swallow Tower. In Chisato's poem, things are seen from the woman's point of view (see *matsu onna*); she lives alone in her quarters with only the moon to visit her.

The influence of Chinese poetry (*kanshi*) is also evident in the use of parallelism: 'a thousand things' (*chiji ni mono*) in the first part of the poem contrasts with 'me alone' (*waga mi hitotsu*) in the second part. Chinese poetry of the Six Dynasties and Tang periods (222–589 and 618–907) exerted an enormous influence on *waka* poetry. The idea that autumn was a sad season is also Chinese in origin.

Oe no Chisato (*fl. c.*889–923) was a courtier and poet. He came from a prominent family of scholars and was the nephew of Ariwara no Yukihira (poem 16) and Narihira (poem 17). Chisato is best remembered today as the author of the *Kudai waka* (*Waka* on Lines from Chinese Poems; 894), known also as the *Chisato-shū* (Chisato Collection), a selection of *waka* based on lines from famous Chinese poems. He has twenty-five poems in the imperial *waka* anthologies.

24

Poem 24 honours the gods of Mount Tamuke (a famous poetic location – see *utamakura*) while also showing the poet's loyalty to the sovereign. Streamers made from unprocessed hemp fibre are used in many Shinto rituals as an offering to the gods or to decorate sacred sites. In place of the streamers, the poet suggests using the beautiful maple leaves of the mountain itself. It is a charming thought that perfectly captures the refined sensibility of Heian aristocrats and their love and admiration of nature. The poem was composed during an imperial progress that Emperor Uda made shortly after abdicating in 897. According to the *Fuso ryakki* (Concise Chronicle of Japan; 1094–1169), Michizane noted in his diary for 23 October 898 that he accompanied the retired emperor to Miyatake and that the poem was written on this occasion.

Shortly after his death, Michizane himself came to be venerated as Kitano Tenjin, the god of learning, and the fact that this was a poem by a god about other gods added to its appeal for later readers.

Sugawara no Michizane (845–903) was a poet, scholar and courtier. Born into a prominent family of Confucian scholars, he quickly rose through the ranks under Emperor Uda (r. 887–97), eventually reaching the office of Minister of the Right and the senior third rank. After Uda's abdication, he fell victim to Fujiwara no Tokihira's political machinations and was appointed Governor of Dazaifu (modern-day Kyushu), which amounted to being exiled. He died there in 903. The numerous calamities that followed his death were attributed to his angry spirit, and efforts to placate him eventually led to his being venerated as the god of learning. Japanese students to this day still earnestly pray to his spirit before exams. He left a sizeable body of work in Chinese (see *kanshi*) and Japanese, including a mixed anthology of Chinese and Japanese poems called the *Shinsen man'yōshū* (New Collection of Ten Thousand Leaves; *c*.893). Sometimes referred to as 'Kanke', which means 'Sugawara Family', he was among the third generation of individuals in the family to use that pseudonym. Zeami's **Noh** play *Oimatsu* (The Ancient Pine), about a pine tree beloved by Michizane, is set in Anrakuji, where the grave of the Sugawara clan is located. The poem here was cited by the great fifteenth-century *renga* master Priest Sogi, in his *Tsukushi no michi no ki*, a travel diary of a pilgrimage to Dazaifu.

25

Rife with puns and double entendres, this is a typical tenth-century love poem. As well as the pun on 'to meet' in the *au* sound of 'Osaka' in Osaka Barrier (see *utamakura* and commentary to poem 10), further wordplay is provided by the words *sa ne* in *sanekazura* (a type of vine), which mean 'let us lie together', and by *kuru*, which can mean both 'to wind', as a creeping vine would do, and 'to come'.

According to the headnote (*kotobagaki*) in the **Gosenshū** (no. 701), the poem was addressed by a man to a woman. If *kuru* in the fifth line is taken to mean 'to come', however, it suggests that the poem would be composed either by a woman or by someone posing as one (see *matsu onna*), as it was women who typically received the visits of lovers, not vice versa.

Fujiwara no Sadakata (873–932) was a prominent poet and courtier, appointed as the Minister of the Right of the Third Ward. The father of Asatada (poem 44), he was also the cousin and father-in-law of Kanesuke (poem 27). Sadakata appears in several stories in **The Tales of Yamato**. He has nineteen poems in the imperial *waka* anthologies, including one in the **Kokinshū** (no. 231), and a private collection of poems.

26

Poem 26 was composed after an imperial outing by the retired Emperor Uda (r. 887–97) to the Oi River (see also poem 24). Because the scenery was so breathtaking, the poet exhorts the current emperor, Uda's son, Daigo (r. 897–930), to also visit the place. Mount Ogura in north-west Kyoto was famous for the beauty of its autumnal foliage (see *utamakura*).

Here the poet addresses a feature of the landscape (the maples) as though it was human. This is not an uncommon device in *waka*; another example is in the *Kokinshū* (no. 832), composed by Kamutsuke no Mineo (*fl.* ninth century) as a funeral elegy for Fujiwara no Mototsune (836–91):

> Dear Cherry Blossoms
> of the Fukakusa Plain,
> if you have a heart
> for just this year,
> please bloom in black!

(Fukakusa no / nobe no sakura shi / kokoro araba / kotoshi bakari wa / sumizome ni sake)

It was common practice among sovereigns and senior members of the court to travel to places of scenic beauty, accompanied by their retainers, and to compose poetry at such locations. Besides their obvious recreational function, these outings served to strengthen the bonds between the members of the court and thus maintain harmony.

Teika himself often accompanied Emperor Gotoba (poem 99) on his frequent excursions, although entries in the poet's diary reveal that he was not always happy to do so and was critical of the various ministers and advisers who supported this over-indulgent lifestyle (see Robert H. Brower and Earl Miner (trans.), *Fujiwara Teika's 'Superior Poems of our Time'* (Stanford, CA: Stanford University Press, 1967), p. 9). It is possible that Teika chose this particular poem because he himself owned a villa on Mount Ogura, as did Rensho, for whom the one hundred poems that eventually became the *One Hundred Poets* were initially selected (see the Introduction, p. xvi).

Fujiwara no Tadahira (880–949), Chancellor of the Realm, was known posthumously as Teishinko (Lord Upright and Faithful). He succeeded his elder brother Tokihira as head of the powerful northern branch (*hokke*) of the Fujiwara clan. Tadahira was Minister of the Left under Emperor Daigo (r. 897–930) and regent (*sesshō*) under Emperor Suzaku (r. 930–46). He has seven poems in the *Gosenshū* and six more in later imperial *waka* anthologies. He also left a journal, the *Teishinkō-ki*.

27

Like poem 25, this love poem is full of wit and rhetorical play. The first three lines up to *Izumigawa* (Izumi River; literally, 'River of Springs') form a preface (*jokotoba*), conjuring up a visual picture that is connected to what follows by the similar-sounding *itsu mi* in line 4. In classical **kana**, the sounds *zu* and *tsu* were written in the same way, so the first part of *Izumigawa* puns with *itsu mi ka* (literally, 'when will I see you?'). To convey the pun in the translation, 'spring' is used in two different senses, 'River of Springs' and 'When did you first *spring* into view?' This is reinforced in the Japanese by *wakite* (to spring) in line 2, an associative word (*engo*) for *izumi* (spring). The sound *mi* is repeated throughout the poem, giving it a strong aural cohesion. 'Field of Jars' is my translation of *Mika no hara*. As Mika is a place name (like the Izumi River, a well-known poetic location – see **utamakura**), it is not usually translated, but the character for it means 'jar' or 'pot'; *hara* is usually translated as 'field' or 'plain'. It is a slightly irregular translation, but poetic, I believe.

Fujiwara no Kanesuke (877–923), a famous courtier and gallant, was known as the Middle Counsellor of the Embankment because his residence was next to the Kamo River. He was the cousin of Sadakata (poem 25) and had a long association with the compilers of the **Kokinshū**, Tsurayuki (poem 35) and Mitsune (poem 29). Kanesuke appears in many of the stories of **The Tales of Yamato**. He has fifty-seven poems in the imperial **waka** anthologies, as well as a private collection. He is one of Kintō's **Thirty-Six Poetic Geniuses**.

28

Poem 28 beautifully conflates natural and human imagery. The word *karu* (in the form *karenu*, 'dried up', in the poem) acts as a pun (*kakekotoba*) meaning both 'to wither' and '[visitors] grow infrequent' that serves to connect the season (winter) to the poet's sense of isolation. The word *yamazato*, translated here as 'mountain abode', can also mean 'mountain hamlet', conveying more of a sense of community and therefore not quite so isolated. The poem is a variation on one by Fujiwara no Okikaze (*fl.* early tenth century):

> When autumn comes
> I join the crickets
> in their plaintive cry,
> for I know grasses and visitors
> will both dry up.

> *(Aki kureba / mushi to tomo ni / nakarenuru /*
> *hito mo kusaba mo / karenu to omoeba)*

In poem 28, the season has changed to winter, which further deepens the sense of physical and emotional withering. In Teika's time, it was the forlorn scenery of both autumn and winter that poets found most affecting, so it is not difficult to see what Teika liked about this poem. He himself composed a variation, which he included in his private collection, *Shūigusō* (The Dull Musings of a Chamberlain; 1216):

> Even on the path of dreams
> visitors have withered
> and frost settles
> on the meadow grasses
> as I pass the night in sleepless wait.

> *(Yumeji made / hitome wa karenu / kusa no hara /*
> *oki akasu shimo ni / musubōretsutsu)*

Minamoto no Muneyuki (d. 939) was a grandson of Emperor Koko (poem 15). After being reduced to commoner status in 894, he held a number of nominal provincial governorships. He was appointed a magistrate in 939, but died shortly afterwards. Muneyuki has fifteen poems in the imperial *waka* anthologies, six of them in the *Kokinshū*, as well as a private collection. He is one of Kinto's **Thirty-Six Poetic Geniuses**.

29

Teika seems to have had a special fondness for white (see the Introduction, p. xxii), so it is not difficult to see what must have impressed him about poem 29. To the poet's eyes, the early-morning frost makes the pure white chrysanthemums all but indistinguishable from the frost itself. The poet's professed inability to tell apart the white chrysanthemums from the whiteness of the frost was something that Heian audiences, following in the footsteps of their Six-Dynasty Chinese predecessors, found irresistibly elegant. Indeed, the poem is a good example of the poetic device of 'elegant confusion' (*mitate*). Teika considered this one of his favourite poems and included it in virtually all of the numerous selections of poetry that he compiled. Common in Chinese poetry (*kanshi*), the chrysanthemum only began to be used in *waka* around the time of the *Kokinshū* (tenth century).

The Meiji poet Masaoka Shiki (1867–1902) rejected this poem, asserting that it was a fabrication based on a lie (*uso no shiko*), but Heian courtiers loved the stylized and unlikely conflation of the first frost and chrysanthemums and praised the image as being of the most refined beauty.

Oshikochi no Mitsune (d. *c*.925). Although he had only a modest career in the imperial bureaucracy, Mitsune was one of the leading poets of his time, and his services were sought by friends and emperors alike. He was one of the compilers of the *Kokinshū*, and with Tsurayuki (poem 35), the best-represented poet in that collection; 196 of his poems were collected in the imperial *waka* anthologies after the *Kokinshū*, including a large number of *byōbu-uta* (poems on screens) and poems from *uta-awase* poem contests. He is one of Kinto's **Thirty-Six Poetic Geniuses**.

30

According to anecdotes in Ichijo Kanera's *Kokinshū dōmōshō* (Glimpses of the *Kokinshū*; 1476) and in the *setsuwa* collection *Kokon chōmonjū* (Collection of Things Written and Heard Then and Now; *c.*1254), Teika and his fellow poet Ietaka (poem 98) were once asked which was the best poem in the **Kokinshū**, and they both had no hesitation in naming this poem by Tadamine. Teika explains his admiration for it in his *Kensho mikkan* (My Views on Kensho's Commentary; 1221): 'The wording and the conceit are so elegant and charming that if one can compose even a single poem like this, one's fame will be guaranteed.'

The original poem in the *Kokinshū* (no. 625) was about returning home in the morning after having been refused audience by a cold-hearted lady. Teika, however, took the word *tsurenaku* (cold-hearted, indifferent) in line 2 to refer specifically to the moon at dawn, heralding the end of a much-awaited encounter, rather than to the lady's attitude, and I have followed his interpretation in the translation. A translation closer to the original meaning of the poem would read:

> Since I parted from you
> nothing is so miserable
> as that time before dawn,
> the look on your face then
> cold as the moon at dawn.

Though dating from the early tenth century, the poem shows some of the elements of the *yōen* style (see the Introduction, pp. xii–xiii) that was in vogue in the **Shin-kokinshū** period, including elegant imagery, romantic subject matter and a tale-like atmosphere.

Mibu no Tadamine (*fl.* 893–920) is one of the four compilers of the *Kokinshū*. Whereas the reputation of other great tenth-century poets somewhat declined in subsequent centuries, Tadamine's remained consistently high. Kinto (poem 55) placed one of his poems in the highest of his *Waka kuhon* (Nine Levels of *Waka*; written after 1009), alongside a poem by the great Hitomaro (poem 3). He has eighty-two poems in the imperial *waka* anthologies, thirty-five of which are in the *Kokinshū* alone, as well as a private collection. His son Tadami (poem 41) was also a distinguished poet.

31

Poem 31 exemplifies the 'elegant confusion' (*mitate*) valued by poets of the era, as the poet struggles to distinguish between the snow covering Mount Yoshino and the light of the moon. *Yoshino no sato* in the original Japanese refers to Yoshino Village, rather that the old capital of Yoshino, though both were situated near Mount Yoshino and all three locations were often cited in poetry (see *utamakura* and commentary to poem 94). The mixture of dazzling visual imagery and evocation of the Yoshino name with its myriad associations gives the poem a timeless, elegiac beauty – precisely the combination that Teika and many of his contemporaries loved.

To see snow as moonlight is like seeing flowers as snow, and both metaphors were commonly used at that time. Both employ the technique of *mitateru*, which was very important in Japanese aesthetics (see *mitate*). This involved substituting one thing for another that had something in common with the original image. Here, the common link is the colour white. In the sixteenth century, this idea was harnessed by the tea master Sen no Rikyu, who would substitute many of the utensils in the tea ceremony for alternatives, to stunning effect (for example, a Korean rice bowl for a tea bowl, as they share the same shape). The literary origins of this was Chinese poetry (*kanshi*), as exemplified by the Tang Dynasty poet Li Bai's famous poem 'Quietly Contemplating at Night', which would have been well known in Japan at the time. I have translated it roughly:

> I gaze upon the moonlight
> at the foot of my bed,
> like white frost,
> then look up at the moon
> above the mountain
> and, lowering my head,
> I remember my home.

Sakanoue no Korenori (d. 930) had a modest career as a minor official, ending as Governor of Kaga (modern-day Ishikawa Prefecture). He won his greatest glory as a master of *kemari* football. He left a private collection and forty poems in the imperial *waka* anthologies, of which eight are in the *Kokinshū*. His son Mochiki (d. *c.*975) was one of the editors of the *Gosenshū*. Korenori is one of Kinto's **Thirty-Six Poetic Geniuses**.

32

The sense of wonder at nature's beauty connects poem 32 to the previous one. Through devices such as personification and 'elegant confusion' (*mitate*), Heian poets blurred the boundaries between the natural and human worlds, achieving a harmonious synthesis. Like poem 29, this poem conflates two elements of the natural world – the built-up leaves and the fishing weir – which in reality are distinct. The auxiliary verb *keri* in the last line (which could be translated as 'ah!') expresses the observer's delighted surprise at his discovery.

According to the preface (*jokotoba*) to the poem as it appears in the *Kokinshū*, the setting is the Shiga Mountain Trail (*Shiga no Yamagoe*). This was famous both as a topic for poems and as a place name (*utamakura*) that was widely invoked in classical poetry. The trail, which led over a mountain in Shiga in Omi Province (modern-day Shiga Prefecture), started from Kitashirakawa in Kyoto, passed through Hieizan and Nyoigatake, then Omi and Otsu, ending at Shiga no Sato. Emperor Tenji (poem 1) established a capital at Shiga no Sato and the place was also the setting or topic of many poems.

Ancient fishing weirs were built by planting large wooden posts into the riverbed and placing bamboo canes horizontally across the posts to help trap the fish.

Harumichi no Tsuraki (d. 920). Very little is known about his life. After graduating from the imperial university, he served as Greater Secretary of Dazaifu. He was appointed Governor of Iki Province in 920, but died before he could take up his new post. Tsuraki has three poems in the *Kokinshū*, and two in the *Gosenshū*.

33

In imperial court culture, cherry blossoms were a symbol of impermanence, and countless poems lament their swift departure, this one being an outstanding example. The scattering was a source of deep

sadness for the sophisticated courtiers of Heian-period Japan, leading
the great poet Narihira (poem 17) to famously exclaim (**Kokinshū**,
no. 53; *The Tales of Ise*, Episode 82):

> If only there were
> no cherry blossoms
> in this world,
> what calm would reign
> in the heart of spring.
>
> *(Yo no naka ni / taete sakura no / nakariseba /
> haru no kokoro wa / nodokekaramashi)*

The reply poem in *The Tales of Ise* argues, however, that it is precisely
because they scatter that they are so precious.

The literary dispute continued into the medieval period. The poet
and memoirist Yoshida Kenko (1283?–1350?) argued in his highly
popular *Tsurezuregusa* (Essays in Idleness; *c*.1332) that the things that
do not last are the most beautiful: 'Are we to look at cherry blossoms
only in full bloom, the moon only when it is cloudless? To long for
the moon while looking on the rain, to lower the blinds and be
unaware of the passing of the spring – these are even more deeply
moving' (*Essays in Idleness: The Tsurezuregusa of Kenkō*, trans. Donald
Keene (New York: Columbia University Press, 1967), p. 115). The
Heian-period love of the frail cherry blossoms fluttering about in the
spring still persists in Japan today, though the association with eva-
nescence has diminished somewhat.

This poem also employs the 'pillow words' (**makura kotoba**) *hisakata
no*, often paired with *hi no hikari* (the light of the sun), here abbreviated
to *hikari* ([sun]light), to heighten the rhetorical effect.

Ki no Tomonori: (d. *c*.905) was a cousin of Tsurayuki (poem 35). He
helped with the compilation of the *Kokinshū*, but died shortly after its
completion (an elegy in his memory appears in it, no. 838). He has
forty-seven poems in the *Kokinshū* and over twenty more in later
imperial *waka* anthologies. He is one of Kinto's **Thirty-Six Poetic
Geniuses**.

34

Poem 34 depicts the sadness of old age through the well-loved meta-phor of the pine tree. The pine was a symbol of long life, and was often used in auspicious poems to express a wish for longevity, though here the association is used negatively to craft a bitter lament on old age. Only the pine of Takasago, the poet notes, is as old as he is but, alas, he is no friend. The pines of Takasago in Harima (modern-day Hyogo Prefecture) and of Sumiyoshi (poem 18) were particularly fam-ous and the location is often referred to in poetry (see *utamakura*). These pines trees are mentioned in the *Kokinshū* preface as the 'paired' (*aioi*) pines. In the **Noh** play *Takasago* by Zeami, they are portrayed as an elderly husband and wife, and symbolize unflinching love and devotion in spite of distance. It is possible, as Shimazu Tadao notes, that the seventy-four-year-old Teika saw his own heart in this poem (*Hyakunin isshu*, 2nd edn (Tokyo: Kadokawa Shoten, 1999), p. 80).

Fujiwara no Okikaze (*fl.* late ninth century) was a prominent mem-ber of the literary circles of the mid Heian period. He participated in numerous poetry competitions and was a reputed *koto* player. He had seventeen poems in the *Kokinshū* and twenty-one in later imperial *waka* anthologies; he also left a private poetry collection. Okikaze is one of Kinto's **Thirty-Six Poetic Geniuses**. The poet is the great-grandchild of Fujiwara no Hamanari (724–90), the author of the first treatise on poetry, *Kakyo hyoshiki* (The Rules of *Waka*; 772).

35

Comparisons between people and nature are often made in *waka*, but in poem 35 the focus is on the contrast between them: whereas people change, nature does not. According to the headnote (*kotoba-gaki*) to the poem in the *Kokinshū* (no. 42), Tsurayuki always stayed with a friend on his way to worship at Hasedera in Hatsuse (a poetic location – see *utamakura* and commentary to poem 74) and was vis-iting after a long break. Hasedera contained a famous sculpture of the Juichimen Kannon (the Bodhisattva of Compassion), and many people worshipped there in the Heian period; it appears often in the literature of the time, including *The Tale of Genji*, as in the scene where Hikaru Genji meets Tamakazura.

To his host's sarcastic remark ('There will always be room for you here'), Tsurayuki apparently responded with this poem. In the Japanese, a strong caesura separates the first two lines, focusing on human experience, and the last three lines, which deal with nature, but this is reflected more gently in the translation.

The plum blossom was especially popular as a poetic topic in the *Man'yōshū* period (seventh and eighth centuries). It continued to be used in the Heian period, but it was supplanted in popularity by cherry blossoms (*sakura*), which became the quintessential spring topic, as reflected in poem 33, for instance. Only the word for 'flower' (*hana*) appears in the original poem, but readers of the period would have understood it to mean plum blossom. One reason for this is that plum blossom, unlike cherry, is always associated with its fragrance. Cherry blossom, by contrast, is associated with its evanescence.

Ki no Tsurayuki (872?–945). One of the foremost poets of the Heian period, he was the chief compiler of the *Kokinshū*, and wrote its famous preface in Japanese. He led the battle to have Japanese poetry regarded as the equal of Chinese poetry (*kanshi*). In 930 he was appointed Governor of Tosa in Shikoku. Assuming the persona of a woman (see **matsu onna**), he wrote a famous diary, the *Tosa nikki* (Tosa Diary; 935), about his return journey from Tosa to the capital. A total of 452 of his poems appear in imperial *waka* anthologies, 102 of them in the *Kokinshū* alone. He has a private collection of poems and is one of Kinto's **Thirty-Six Poetic Geniuses**.

36

Under the influence of Chinese poetry (*kanshi*), mid Heian poets looked for elegant and witty ways to describe the beauty of nature, as in this poem that celebrates the moon. Summer nights were by definition short and left little time to admire the beauty of the moon. In the poem the moon is personified: the summer night is so short that it cannot reach the western horizon where it usually sets, leaving the poet to wonder behind which cloud it will spend the day. Traditionally the moon was used to express autumn, so its use here for summer is fresh and original, and there is a hint of humour in how it has been personified.

Kiyohara no Fukayabu (*fl.* ninth/tenth centuries) was a descendant of Prince Toneri, the founder of Nara, grandfather of Motosuke (poem 42) and the great-grandfather of Sei Shonagon (poem 62). The late-Heian poet and critic Kiyosuke (poem 84) ranked him a first-class poet, on a par with Kinto's **Thirty-Six Poetic Geniuses**. Forty-one of Fukayabu's poems were included in imperial *waka* anthologies, including seventeen in the *Kokinshū* alone.

37

This poem deploys a particularly characteristic rhetorical device to add freshness and wit to its description of nature: 'elegant confusion' (*mitate*), or mistaking one thing for another (the dew for gems). A dew-covered field is imagined as being where gems from a necklace that had not been secured properly have scattered. The poem can be considered a variation on, or a companion poem to, *Kokinshū* no. 225, also by Asayasu:

> Are those white dewdrops pearls
> spread upon the autumn fields?
> They are linked
> by the silken threads
> of a spider's web.

> *(Aki no no ni / oku shiratsuyu wa / tama nareya /
> tsuranukikakuru / kumo no ito suji)*

The poem above chiefly differs from poem 37 in that it also uses personification – the spider fabricating a necklace from the 'pearls' of dew.

Fun'ya no Asayasu (*fl.* ninth/tenth centuries) or Bun'ya no Asayasu/ Tomoyasu, a low-ranking official, was the son of the more famous Yasuhide (poem 22), one of the **Six Poetic Geniuses**. Asayasu participated in many poetry competitions and three of his poems appear in imperial *waka* anthologies.

38

Poem 38 appears in Episode 84 of *The Tales of Yamato* as a poem sent
to a man who had forgotten about the author despite his numerous
promises. Though many tenth-century court romances are light in
tone, the 'how I fear for you' in line 3 could be read as a veiled threat
to the forgetful lover – people at the time believed that if you did not
keep a promise made before the gods, you would incur divine wrath –
or simply light sarcasm. Teika, however, seems to have found the
idea of caring for someone even after having been hurt by them
deeply moving. And indeed the poem is imbued with a complex mix-
ture of love and hate. Teika composed a poem clearly based on this
one in his *Shūigusō* (The Dull Musings of a Chamberlain; 1216), no.
2078:

> For love I was ready
> to give up my life,
> so how I fear for you.
> Don't you remember
> the vow that made us one?

> *(Mi o sutete / hito no inochi o / oshimu to mo /*
> *arishi chikai no / oboe yawa sen)*

Ukon (*fl.* tenth century) was the daughter or younger sister of Suenawa,
Captain of the Imperial Guard of the Left, who was said to be the
model of a famous gallant in the no longer extant *Katano no shosho* (The
Tale of Katano no Shosho). Ukon also had pronounced amorous pro-
clivities and *The Tales of Yamato* recount several of her love affairs with
Fujiwara nobles and others. She was a lady-in-waiting to Empress
Onshi, consort to Emperor Daigo (r. 897–930). Nine of her poems
appear in the imperial *waka* anthologies.

39

With the next pair of poems (40 and 41), poem 39 forms a triptych
on concealed love. Courtly love in Heian-period Japan followed a

predetermined pattern: it began with one of the two lovers secretly falling for the other, followed by exchanges of poems (*zōtōka*), the long wait for a chance to meet and a phase of secret encounters, and ended unhappily with the eventual estrangement of the lovers. This poem focuses on the early phase, when the lover has yet to reveal or is in the process of revealing his feelings.

The first part of the poem is a preface (*jokotoba*), which is connected to the rest by the repetition of *shino* in *shinohara* (literally, the 'plain of low bamboo') and *shinoburedo* (I try to conceal my feelings). This is an example of a preface that is based on sound play (see also the commentary to poem 51). Prefaces are sometimes related semantically to the main meaning of the poem, though often, as in this example, they merely fulfil an ornamental function. Here, there is also a connection in terms of the imagery, with the reeds that are hidden in the low bamboo and the feelings that are too great to hide. This is reflected in the playful translation, where the bold letters spell 'they show'. The repetition of the *shi* sound – *shinohara*, *shinoburedo*, *koishiki* – creates a beautiful aural effect.

Minamoto no Hitoshi (880–951) was the great-grandson of Emperor Saga (r. 809–23). After serving as governor of several important provinces, in 947 he was appointed counsellor of the fourth rank. Four of his poems appear in the *Gosenshū*.

40

Many of the poems in the collection form pairs. The reason is that the poems that eventually came to constitute the *One Hundred Poems* are thought to have been originally selected by Teika for the sliding doors of the country villa belonging to his father-in-law Rensho, and at least some of them were initially chosen to appear in pairs on the same panel or doors (see the Introduction, p. xvi). Poems 40 and 41 are one such pair. Both poems were composed for the Poetry Contest of the Fourth Year of Tentoku at the Imperial Palace in 960, one of the most prestigious contests of the Heian period. The event was hosted by Emperor Murakami (r. 946–67) in his living quarters, and became famous as the grandest event of its kind in the tenth century. Both poems also appear next to each other in the *Shūishū* (nos. 621 and 622), the third of the official *waka* anthologies.

This pairing was very important for the Japanese and they loved to judge which was the best of the two. Incidentally, although poem 39 is similar in theme to nos. 40 and 41, the link is not as strong since it was not composed for the same poetry contest, and was not placed subsequently with these poems in other anthologies.

Love is the theme of both poems, and both focus on the early stage of the romance, when the lovers are still trying to keep their love secret and rumours are just beginning to spread. Poem 40 is marvellously straightforward: despite the poet's best efforts to conceal it, his love for an unknown mistress shows in his face.

Taira no Kanemori (910?–990) was a descendant of Emperor Koko (poem 15) and a court official who ended his career as Governor of Suruga. He was also one of the most respected poets of his generation. When Kinto (poem 55) compiled his selection of poems by **Thirty-Six Poetic Geniuses**, Kanemori was one of only six poets to have ten of their poems included, the other five being Hitomaro (poem 3), Tsurayuki (poem 35), Mitsune (poem 29), Ise (poem 19) and Kanemori's contemporary Nakatsukasa (912–91). Eighty-seven of his poems appear in the imperial *waka* anthologies and three poems given as 'anonymous' in the *Gosenshū* are considered to be his.

41

This poem forms a pair with poem 40 and, like that one, focuses on the gossip that invariably grew around a love affair meant to be kept secret. There were a number of reasons to keep an affair secret in Heian times, the foremost being the difference in rank between the two lovers. Forbidden love with a woman of much higher status provides the main narrative motif for some of the most famous works of Heian-period literature, including *The Tales of Ise* and *The Tale of Genji*.

Like the previous poem, this one was composed for the prestigious Poetry Contest of the Fourth Year of Tentoku at the Imperial Palace in 960. The judge of the event, Fujiwara no Saneyori (900–970), found it hard to choose between the two poems and only awarded the victory to Kanemori's poem because the emperor was overheard reciting the poem to himself. Later critics, however, agreed in rating Tadami's poem far superior. Indeed, the poem masterfully sets up a contrast in the first part between the outer world (society's view of the lovers, the spread of rumours) and, in the last part, the inner workings of the poet's mind at the beginning of the affair. In the translation, the order is reversed.

According to an anecdote in the medieval collection *Shasekishū* (Collection of Sand and Pebbles; 1283), Tadami was so disappointed by his defeat at the Tentoku contest that he stopped eating and died shortly afterwards as a result.

Mibu no Tadami (*fl.* mid tenth century), son of the famous Tadamine (poem 30), was a reputed poet in his own right. Little is known of his career other than that he was appointed Grand Controller of the Province of Settsu. Thirty-six poems of his appear in the imperial *waka* anthologies and there is a private collection of his verse. He is one of Kinto's **Thirty-Six Poetic Geniuses**.

42

Like poem 38, this one is also about broken vows. The association of the place name Mount Sue no Matsu (see *utamakura*) with everlasting love dates back at least as far as the early tenth century, as exemplified by this poem from the *Kokinshū* (no. 1093), which is credited with having started the trend:

> Though it would never happen,
> if my heart were so fickle
> as to leave you
> the waves would swallow
> the Mount of Vows . . .

> *(Kimi o okite / adashi gokoro no / ware moteba /*
> *Sue no matsuyama / nami mo kosanan)*

The image is based on the idea that Mount Sue no Matsu was so high that it was impossible for the waves to rise high enough to cover it and equally for the lover to break his vows. Its name in Japanese, *Sue no Matsuyama*, literally means 'Pine Tree Mountain Without End'. In the poem above, I have translated it as 'Mount of Vows' for its special association with the making of vows in love poetry; in poem 42 it is translated as 'Mount of Forever-Green Pines', punning on 'loving for*ever*' and '*ever*-green', with 'ever' acting as a **pivot word** in English (but not in the original Japanese).

The last line of the translation is only implied in the original; the poem could otherwise be rendered with the final line left blank for the reader to fill in:

> Wringing tears from our sleeves,
> did we not pledge never to part –
> not even if the waves engulfed
> the Mount of Forever-Green Pines
> ....?

The broken syntax of the poem adds immediacy and gives it a nice conversational quality. In the original, the break occurs at the end of the first line, which would read: 'Did we not make vows –' (*Chigiriki-na*); in the translation, the break occurs after the second line.

Kiyohara no Motosuke (908–90), grandson of Fukayabu (poem 36) and father of Sei Shonagon (poem 62), was one of the most important poets of the tenth century. He served as an official in various provinces. In 951, he assisted in the compilation of the *Gosenshū* and transcription of the *Man'yōshū*. One of Kinto's **Thirty-Six Poetic Geniuses**, he was the author of a voluminous private poetry collection and more than one hundred poems in the imperial *waka* anthologies.

43

Poem 43 is an example of a 'morning-after poem' (*kinuginu no uta*), sent by a man to reassure his beloved after a night spent together. Here the poet reassures the lady that his feelings are no less intense than they were before it (see also poems 50 and 80). Sending a morning-after poem was part of the complex code of conduct followed by Heian aristocratic lovers, and failure to send one, regardless of whether one intended to continue the relationship or not, would have been considered extremely impolite. Sometimes it was the woman who sent such notes, to express her feelings (as in poem 80), solicit a response or to chastise an inattentive lover.

Fujiwara no Atsutada (906–43), third son of the powerful Fujiwara minister Tokihira (871–909), was a renowned musician and also known for his beauty. There are tales of his amorous escapades in many books, including *The Tales of Yamato*. Thirty poems by him appear in the official *waka* anthologies and he also has a private collection of poetry. He is one of Kinto's **Thirty-Six Poetic Geniuses.**

44

Like poems 40 and 41, this one was also composed at the Poetry Contest of the Fourth Year of Tentoku at the Imperial Palace in 960. The theme is also love, but the tone is much darker than in the previous poems. It is not clear, based on the original wording, if the encounter between the lovers has taken place or not, and the overall impression of the poem changes considerably depending on how one decides to read it. Judging from where Teika placed it in his digest of the first eight imperial *waka* collections (*Hachidaishō*; 1215–16), he probably read it as an 'after-the-encounter' poem, and so I have followed this interpretation in my translation. The underlying message of the poem is that the encounters that lovers so yearn for are in fact the cause of their suffering. The poem is often mentioned in medieval commentaries as a love poem that does not mention the word 'love' (*koi*), but this cannot be conveyed so easily in translation, hence I have included the word here.

Nakanaka in line 3 does not mean 'very' or 'considerably', as it does in modern Japanese, but 'on the contrary' or 'instead'. In the translation, it is rendered 'If we had never'.

Fujiwara no Asatada (910–66), aka Tomotada, was the fifth son of Sadakata (poem 25) and a Middle Counsellor. In his time, he was considered one of the finest poets of his generation, although his reputation somewhat declined over time. He was also a well-known gallant. Twenty-one poems of his appear in the official *waka* anthologies and he is one of Kinto's **Thirty-Six Poetic Geniuses.**

45

Although readers of classical Japanese literature may be more familiar with the topic of the heartbroken lady, men were also cast off by estranged lovers as often as women were. In poem 45 it is the man who vents his despair at having been forgotten by his beloved. The head-note (*kotobagaki*) to the poem as it appears in the *Shūishū* (no. 950) simply reads: 'He composed the poem when a woman with whom he had started an affair subsequently became cold and eventually stopped seeing him altogether.' The author, Koremasa, was the archetypical 'amorous gentleman' (*irogonomi*) of the mid tenth century. His many romantic exploits are recorded in the *Ichijō sesshō gyoshū* (Collection of His Highness, the Regent of the First Ward; *c.*972), a heavily fictional-ized collection of love stories based on his own poems that he is believed to have edited himself.

Fujiwara no Koremasa (924–72), aka Fujiwara no Koretada, known posthumously as Kentoku-ko (Lord Humble and Virtuous), was a high-ranking courtier. The son of the prominent statesman Morosuke, he held numerous important offices, eventually becoming regent in 970. At the age of twenty-six, he was appointed superintendent of the editorial committee that compiled the *Gosenshū*. In addition to the *Ichijō sesshō gyoshū*, thirty-seven of his poems appear in the official *waka* anthologies.

46

One of the loveliest poems in the collection, this is another example of a poem that employs imagery from the natural world to express a sentiment, using a famous place name, the Bay of Yura (see *utam-akura*), to give added resonance. The first three lines form a preface (*jokotoba*) ending in a **pivot phrase** that connects the first part of the poem ('The boat is adrift / *not knowing where it goes*') with the second ('*not knowing where it goes* / Is the course of love [also] like this?'). A view of the landscape is thus sketched which is then linked to the message of the poem: like the course of a boat that has lost its rudder, the way of love is filled with uncertainty.

Sone no Yoshitada (*fl.* mid-to-late tenth century) was one of the most original poets of his time. Not much is known about him except that he was a secretary (*jo*) in Tango Province, hence his sobriquets Sotango and Sotan. Whereas most of his contemporaries preferred safe, manneristic compositions in the style of the *Kokinshū*, he is known for his daring, sometimes outrageous poems, in which he often employs archaic diction and imagery. He seems to have been an eccentric character and in time he became something of a comic figure, mocked in a wealth of anecdotes and stories dating from the late Heian period onwards. Eighty-nine poems of his appear in imperial *waka* anthologies later than the *Shūishū*. He also wrote the *Yoshitada hyakushu* (*c.*961), the first example on record of a one-hundred-poem sequence (*hyakushu*).

47

Like poem 35, this poem contrasts the fickle human heart with the unchanging cyclical rhythm of nature: although visitors have stopped coming, autumn never fails to visit. The arrival of autumn, however, brings little comfort to the poet and only makes the sense of loneliness and isolation from the world more acute. According to the headnote (*kotobagaki*) to the poem in the *Shūishū* (no. 140), it was composed on the theme 'autumn comes to the ruined villa', based on the ruins of the once-splendid Kawara-in residence built by Minamoto no Toru (poem 14). After Toru's death it became a site of pilgrimage for poets, and poetry gatherings were often hosted there. Thus the melancholia evoked by the poem is not to be taken as the poet's own, but rather as a poetic distillation of the theme of loneliness, which in many ways anticipates the medieval ideal of *yūgen* (see the Introduction, p. xii). *Yaemugura* in the first line of the Japanese is a general term for creeping vines and weeds that overgrow an abandoned garden.

Priest Egyo (*fl.* second half of the tenth century) often participated in poetry gatherings with fellow poets Motosuke (poem 42), Shigeyuki (poem 48) and Yoshinobu (poem 49). Fifty-six of his poems appear in the *Shūishū* and later imperial *waka* anthologies. He has a private collection of poems.

48

This is a love poem of rare power and inventiveness. Swept by strong winds, the waves furiously hit the rocks, only to be shattered by them, much like the heart of a suitor who pursues an unresponsive lover. Like the previous poem, it employs the device of a preface (*jokotoba*), in which a description of the landscape in the first part of the poem doubles up as a metaphor of the poet's feelings. The word *kudakeru* is both a **pivot word** and a pun (*kakekotoba*) with the double meaning of 'my heart breaks' and the 'waves crash'.

The preface consists of the words up to '*kaze o itami / iwa utsu nami no.*' Then the words '*onore nomi*' separate it from the words it modifies, '*kudakete mono o.*' We can see from this that the preface does not need to be directly attached to the words it modifies.

Minamoto no Shigeyuki (d. *c.*1000) was a major poet of his time. Despite being a great-grandson of Emperor Seiwa (r. 857–76), he held mostly minor posts at court and in the provincial bureaucracy. He seems to have been the first to compose a one-hundred-poem sequence (*hyakushū*), which became a very popular format in subsequent times (see also the Introduction, p. xxi). Kinto (poem 55) listed him among his **Thirty-Six Poetic Geniuses**. Sixty-seven of Shigeyuki's poems were included in the imperial *waka* anthologies.

49

Poem 49 features a classic pun (*kakekotoba*) based on the word for 'fire' (*hi*), which also appears as the last two letters of the word for 'love' (*omohi*): the poet's love is like the watchman's fire that wanes by day but burns during the night. Societal rules were imposed to keep feelings hidden from view, but in the reassuring secrecy of the night one was free to give full expression to one's emotions by sending passionate notes or visiting a lover. Though attributed to Yoshinobu, the poem does not appear in his collected poems and a version with only minor differences is listed as 'anonymous' in the *Kokin waka rokujō* (Old and New *Waka* in Six Volumes) from the latter part of the tenth century.

Ōnakatomi no Yoshinobu (921–91) was the son of the prominent *Kokinshū*-period poet Yorimoto (*c.*886–958). He was Hereditary High Official of the Department of Religious Affairs. As a member of the Bureau of Poetry, he participated in the transcription of the *Man'yōshū* and compilation of the *Gosenshū*. A total of 126 of his poems appear in the imperial *waka* anthologies. He also has a large private poetry collection and is one of Kintō's **Thirty-Six Poetic Geniuses**.

50

This is another example of a morning-after poem (*kinuginu no uta*). Its conceit – the willingness to die for love transformed, after meeting one's beloved, into a wish to live for ever – is clever, though not to the point of making the poem feel affected or inauthentic. Its headnote (*kotobagaki*) in the *Goshūishū* (no. 669) reads: 'He sent this poem upon returning home from the lady's house.' Love affairs between Heian aristocrats revolved around the exchange of poems (*zōtōka*). They often began with a poem dashed off in haste and could continue for some time until the much-anticipated meeting between the lovers arrived. According to the custom of the time, the visits would continue secretly for three nights. On the morning of the fourth day, the suitor would then reveal himself to the parents of the girl and the couple would be considered married.

Fujiwara no Yoshitaka (954–74), son of Koretada (poem 45), was appointed Captain of the Imperial Guard of the Right. He was the father of the renowned calligrapher Yukinari (972–1027), who was born when Yoshitaka was only eighteen. Yoshitaka died of smallpox at the age of twenty, on the same day as his twin brother. A devout Buddhist, according to the *Ōkagami* (The Great Mirror; *c.*1119), his last wish was that he not be cremated, so that he could come back to life to finish reading the *Lotus Sutra*. His mother ignored his request, however, and his body was cremated, as a result of which he reappeared in a dream and reproached her: 'You promised to bury me but burned me in the end, how could you have forgotten?' After that, he is said to have lived in heaven for eternity, rather than coming back to earth, as he had wished. Twelve of Yoshitaka's poems appear in the official *waka* anthologies; he also has a private collection and is counted among the **Thirty-Six Poetic Geniuses of the Late Classical Period.**

51

As with poems 49 and 50, an image of burning passion lies at the heart of this poem. The poet is unable to express his feelings openly and so his love must burn secretly and slowly like the dried leaves of the moxa plant. Powdered Japanese mugwort or moxa (*Artemesia princeps*) was and is still used as a natural health remedy in East Asian medicine to treat a variety of ailments. Heating certain areas of the body by applying burning moxa leaves (a process known as moxibustion) is believed to have therapeutic effects.

A number of puns (**kakekotoba**) make the poem rhetorically intricate: the verb *iu* ('to say', spelled *ihu* in ancient **kana**) puns on Ibuki (rendered 'Ihuki' in the ancient style); Ibuki in Shiga Prefecture was a poetic location (see **utamakura**) known for mugwort; the word *sashimogusa* (another common name for the moxa plant) puns on *sashimo* ('that much' or 'in this way'); *omoi* (love) puns on *hi* (fire), based on its original spelling of *omohi*; and *moyuru* (to burn) is an associative word (**engo**) for *sashimogusa*. The wordplay on *sashimogusa* and *sashimo* also constitutes a preface (**jokotoba**), linking the first and second parts of the poem. (See also commentary to poem 75 for a differing use of mugwort as an image.)

Fujiwara no Sanekata (d. 998), great-grandson of Tadahira (poem 26), was Commander of the Imperial Guard. In 995, he was appointed Governor of Mutsu (present-day Aomori), where he died. He is cited as a lover of Sei Shonagon (poem 62). A story in the *Kōjidan* (Reminiscing on Old Times; 1212–15) relates that in 995 Emperor Ichijo (r. 986–1011) exiled Sanetaka to the northern province of Mutsu after an argument at court between him and the calligrapher Fujiwara no Yukinari (972–1027). Because Sanekata was well known as an accomplished poet, the emperor is reported to have quipped sarcastically to him, 'Go and visit some poetic locations!' Sixty-eight poems of his appear in the imperial **waka** anthologies. He also left a private poetry collection.

52

Because it marked the moment of separation between lovers, the coming of dawn is lamented in countless love poems, including this one. The headnote (*kotobagaki*) to the poem in the *Goshūishū* (no. 672) says that it was 'sent on returning home, having left the house of a lady on a day the snow was falling', and although the snow is not mentioned in the poem, we can picture the elegant scene of a beautifully dressed courtier leaving the house of his beloved at dawn as the snow quietly falls.

Fujiwara no Michinobu (972–94), son of the statesman Tamemitsu (942–92), was adopted by his powerful uncle Kaneie (see commentary to poem 53). Despite dying young, at the age of twenty-two, he was considered a brilliant commander of the Imperial Guard and had already established a reputation as a fine poet. Forty-nine poems of his are included in the imperial *waka* anthologies. He left a private collection of poems and was listed as one of the **Thirty-Six Poetic Geniuses of the Late Classical Period**.

53

Of all the insensitive husbands at the Heian court, Fujiwara no Kaneie is perhaps the most notorious. The progressive deterioration of his marriage to the woman known to us as the Mother of Michitsuna, his affairs with other women and the suffering this caused his wife are described in wonderful detail in her *Kagerō nikki* (literally, 'The Mayfly Diary', also known as 'The Gossamer Years'; *c.*974), a masterpiece of Heian prose literature. According to this work, poem 53 was composed when Kaneie returned home early one morning having spent the night at the house of another woman. Full of grief and resentment, the Mother of Michitsuna refused to let him in and sent him this poem with a faded chrysanthemum – a reference to the man's change of heart – attached to it. The *Shūishū*, in which the poem was later anthologized (no. 912), tells a somewhat different story: when he returned home one morning, Kaneie waited for a long time for the gate to be opened, until he eventually sent word, saying, 'My legs are sore from standing,' to which his wife replied with this poem. Teika no doubt liked it for the straightforward yet powerful expression of grief.

Mother of Michitsuna (937–95) was a Fujiwara lady noted for her exceptional beauty and mastery of poetry. Secondary consort of Kaneie (929–90), chancellor and regent, she is mainly remembered as the author of *Kagerō nikki*. Her real name is not known, though, somewhat ironically, her son Michitsuna is mostly famous for being related to her. Thirty-nine of her poems appear in the official *waka* anthologies and she also has a private poetry collection. She is listed as one of both the **Thirty-Six Poetic Geniuses of the Late Classical Period** and the **Thirty-Six Women Poetic Geniuses**.

54

Happy endings are rare in Heian court romances, and even happy unions were expected not to last; thus lovers were cautious in the rare and short-lived moments of bliss. Poem 54 forecasts the ultimate failure of the romance, while simultaneously being a rare celebration of present happiness. The nervous, inarticulate phrasing of the original – the natural order of the words in Japanese is inverted in several places – is perfectly suited to expressing the passionate message the poem aims to convey.

A similar sentiment can be found in this poem by Akazome-emon (*c*.960–*c*.1041) – a contemporary of the author of poem 54 and also a prominent poet – from the *Goshūishū* (no. 59):

> As I'm so sure
> I will be forgotten
> when tomorrow comes,
> let me die today
> before we have to part.

(Asu naraba / wasuraruru mi ni / narinubeshi / kyō o sugusanu / inochi to mogana)

Mother of Honorary Grand Minister (d. 996), Takashina no Takako, was the wife of the Grand Chancellor Michitaka (953–95). She had several illustrious children, including the future Empress Teishi (whom

Sei Shonagon, poem 62, served as a lady-in-waiting) and Fujiwara no Korechika (974–1010), who after briefly holding the position of Minister of the Right was forced out of office by his uncle Michinaga, and given the grandiloquent but empty new title of Honorary Grand Minister.

55

Kinto was considered the best poet of his generation and poems such as this one help to explain how he earned his reputation. Although the water no longer 'flows' (*nagare*), the 'reputation' (*na*) of the place as a marvellous site is still 'passed down' (also *nagare*; rendered *nagarete* in the poem) from one generation to another. The repetition of *na* sounds in the second part of the poem and of *ta* – *taki* (waterfall) and *tae* ('dry up'; rendered *taete* in the poem) – in the first two lines calls to mind the continuous falling water, which miraculously seems to flow in language even though the actual water has dried up. The translation employs a visual layout of short lines to express a sense of the flow of the waterfall. A five-line version would read:

> The waterfall dried up
> in the distant past
> and makes not a sound,
> but its fame flows on and on
> and echoes still today.

We know from information in Kinto's private poetry collection that the poem was composed during an excursion to a famous recreational area west of Kyoto where Emperor Saga (r. 809–23) built a magnificent villa and garden in the early ninth century. The waterfall in the poem may refer either to a dried-up waterfall or to a 'dry waterfall' (*karedaki*) created in the garden. The latter is still visible today at the Ozawa pond of the Daikakuji Temple.

Fujiwara no Kinto (966–1041) was the son of the Grand Minister Yoritada (924–89). He held the office of Major Counsellor, but after the death of his daughter he entered religion and retired to a valley in the hills to the north of Kyoto. His home became a Mecca for the best poets and minds of his day, who all deferred to his judgement in

matters poetic. He was involved in the editing of the *Shūishū* and was
the sole editor of the *Wakan rōeishū* (Collection of Chinese and Japa-
nese Poems to Sing; *c.*1018?). He also wrote treatises on the art of
poetry and drew up the first and most famous of the many lists of
Thirty-Six Poetic Geniuses (see also the Introduction, p. xxvii). He
left a considerable body of critical writings and poetry in both Chin-
ese and Japanese. Eighty-nine of his poems were included in the
imperial *waka* anthologies and he left a private collection of poetry.

56

Whereas the previous poem is calm, controlled and elegantly charm-
ing, poem 56 by Izumi Shikibu is spontaneous, passionate and deeply
moving, as her best poems often are. The headnote (*kotobagaki*) to
the poem in the *Goshūishū* (no. 763) states that it was composed
when Izumi was ill. Although the reference to the poet's imminent
death may be a rhetorical exaggeration, it adds pathos to the poem
and makes it more memorable.

In the original Japanese, the powerful first line (*Arazaran*) is blunt
and disconnected from the rest, providing a truly memorable open-
ing to this poem, which may be translated thus:

> I will soon be gone –
> let me take one last memory
> of this world with me.
> May I see you once more,
> may I see you now?

In the main translation, the caesura is moved from the end of the first
line to end of the third, transferring the emphasis from the somewhat
sentimental 'I will soon be gone' to the urgent immediacy of 'May
I see you once, / may I see you now?'

Izumi Shikibu (b. *c.*976–8) was the daughter of Oe no Masamune, Gov-
ernor of Echizen (present-day Fukui), and wife of Tachibana no
Michisada, Governor of Izumi (present-day Osaka Fu). Her daughter
was Ko Shikibu (poem 60). She had an affair with Prince Tametaka, and
then Prince Atsumichi. Like Murasaki Shikibu (poem 57), she served as
a lady-in-waiting to Empress Shoshi (988–1074) and contributed to the

creation of a lively literary salon. She is considered by many to have been the greatest woman poet of the Heian period, a time when supremely talented women flourished. Teika himself was a great admirer of her poetry and included thirty-seven of her poems in his *Hachidaishō* (Selection from the First Eight *Waka* Anthologies; 1215–16). A total of 250 of her poems appear in the imperial *waka* anthologies, and she has two private poetry collections. She is one of both the **Thirty-Six Poetic Geniuses of the Late Classical Period** and the **Thirty-Six Women Poetic Geniuses.**

57

Like Izumi Shikibu (poem 56), *The Tale of Genji* author Murasaki Shikibu belongs to a generation of women poets who laboured to find a personal voice within the conventions established by earlier poets. Poem 57 is ostensibly about the moon, but is in fact a message to a childhood friend the poet had not seen for a long time who had suddenly called for a short visit. The headnote (*kotobagaki*) to the poem in the *Shin-kokinshū* (no. 1497) reads: 'On the tenth night of the seventh month, after the briefest of visits, a childhood friend she had not seen for years was about to leave as the moon shone brightly.' In the original Japanese, only the moon is referred to, but the translation makes clear that it is the friend to whom the poem is actually addressed.

Murasaki Shikibu (*c.*978–*c.*1014) served as a lady-in-waiting to Empress Shoshi (988–1074). A prolific poet, she is most famous as the author of the prose masterpiece *The Tale of Genji*. She also left a diary, *Murasaki Shikibu nikki*, covering the years 1008 to 1010, and a private collection of her poems. She has fifty-eight poems in the official *waka* anthologies and is listed among both the **Thirty-Six Poetic Geniuses of the Late Classical Period** and the **Thirty-Six Women Poetic Geniuses.**

58

Poem 58 was composed as a reply to a man who had accused the poet of having forgotten him (no. 709 in the *Goshūishū*). The word *soyo* in the fourth line means 'that's right' or 'I told you so' ('I swear of my love' in the translation); it also sounds similar to *soyo soyo*, an onomatopoeic evocation of the gentle sound of the wind rustling through the leaves that accompanies the poet's message to her beloved: 'I have never stopped loving you!' Though the focus of the poem is on sound (onomatopoeia and sibilance), the visual aspect is also well developed (the mountain, the wind blowing through the bamboo grove). The translation attempts to retain something of the aural qualities of the original in the use of the closely connected sounds in 'low', 'wind', 'whispers' and 'swear'. Mount Arima and Ina are in the Province of Settsu and both are famous poetic locations (see *utamakura*).

Daini no Sanmi (b. *c.*999), aka Fujiwara no Katako, was the daughter of Murasaki Shikibu (poem 57) and Fujiwara no Nobutaka, and the wet nurse of Emperor Go-Reizei (r. 1045–68). Some commentaries attribute to her the final ten chapters of *The Tale of Genji* but there is no evidence for this claim. Thirty-seven of her poems appear in the imperial *waka* anthologies and she also has a private poetry collection.

59

Whereas love poems expressing resentment (*urami*) usually focus on the suffering and dejection caused by the cold-hearted partner, this is a gentle poem that reveals the poet's disappointment after waiting up all night for her lover to come. The scholar Ishida Yoshisada comments upon 'the progression through the emotional stages – waiting, despair, resentment, sadness, exhaustion – combined with the inexpressible beauty of the moon sinking in the Western sky' and how these 'perfectly embody Teika's aesthetic sense' (quoted in Shimazu, *Hyakunin isshu*, p. 130).

A similar poem was composed by Teika's contemporary and close affiliate Fujiwara no Ryokei (poem 91) and appears as no. 130 in the *Shokukokinshū*, another of the imperial *waka* anthologies.

Could one go straight to sleep?
From behind the mountain,
I wait anxiously
for the moon to appear
above the blossoms.

*(Yasurawade / nenamu monokawa / yama no ha ni /
izayou tsuki o / hana ni machitsutsu)*

Akazome Emon (*c.*960–*c.*1041) was lady-in-waiting to Empress Sho-shi (988–1074) at the same time as Izumi Shikibu (poem 56) and Murasaki Shikibu (poem 57). Murasaki gives a rather flattering account of Emon's poetic prowess in her diary, *Murasaki Shikibu nikki*. She is believed to be the author or co-author of the historical tale *Eiga monogatari* (A Tale of Flowering Fortunes) from the first half of the eleventh century. Ninety-three of her poems appear in the imperial *waka* anthologies and she has a private poetry collection. Akazome Emon is one of both the **Thirty-Six Poetic Geniuses of the Late Classical Period** and the **Thirty-Six Women Poetic Geniuses**.

60

Like the previous poem, poem 60 combines private events and cos-mic imagery to achieve a majestic effect from inconsequential subject matter. According to the headnote (*kotobagaki*) in the *Kin'yōshū* (no. 550), Koshikibu no Naishi wrote this poem, one of the most brilliant in the *One Hundred Poets*, when teased that she could not write one without the help of her mother, the famous poet Izumi Shikibu (poem 56). It is a devastating retort, full of puns and word associa-tions that firmly denies the allegations but somehow also manages to convey a poignancy regarding the great distance separating mother and daughter.

The place name Ikuno puns on *iku* ('to go' or 'to leave') linking Mount Oe and the road: *Ōeyama / Ikuno michi* ('The road that goes [via Ikuno] to Mount Oe'). A second pun revolves around *fumi*, which means both 'letter' and 'to set foot in'. The fourth line in the Japanese therefore means both 'I have yet to set foot in . . .' and 'No letter has come . . .' All this helps to bring out the central message of the poem of 'going it alone', in the sense of the poet composing on her own, which is conveyed in the second line of the translation by 'nor have I sought help with this poem'.

The poem is given added resonance by the reference to no less than three famous place names (*utamakura*) – Mount Oe, Ikuno and Ama no Hashidate. All three places must be passed through to reach the mother's house in Tango (modern-day northern Kyoto Prefecture). Ama no Hashidate, one of the most scenic locations in Japan, literally means the Bridge to Heaven; I have translated it here to convey the sense of distance, metaphorical as much as physical, between the poet and her mother. (The map on p. 244 gives some idea of the actual distance between the three locations.)

Much of the meaning of the poem can only be understood with a knowledge of the context. Translated literally, the original runs something like this:

> As they are so far away
> I have not set foot on Mount Oe
> nor have I received a letter
> from the Bridge to Heaven.

In other words, there is no mention of the accusation that the mother helped to write the poem, nor that, because of the distance between them, it would have been impossible.

Koshikibu no Naishi (d. 1025) was the daughter of Tachibana no Michisada and Izumi Shikibu (poem 56), and, like her mother, a lady-in-waiting to Empress Shoshi (988–1074). She had a son by the Grand Chancellor, Norimichi. Koshikibu died before she was thirty and has just four poems in the imperial *waka* anthologies.

61

Poem 61 amply displays the genius and wit of Ise no Taifu. The *yaezakura*, or eightfold cherry blossom, is a late-blooming variety for which Nara is famous. According to the headnote (*kotobagaki*) to the poem in Ise no Taifu's *Collected Poems* an eightfold cherry blossom was presented to the imperial court by a bishop from Nara. The famous poet Murasaki Shikibu (poem 57) deferred to Ise no Taifu, who then accepted the blossom on behalf of the court. Thereupon the great Fujiwara no Michinaga, Chancellor of the Realm, insisted a poem must be written, so Ise no Taifu dashed off this stunning impromptu piece and thereby proved her genius. In classical Japanese, 'eightfold' is a code for 'splendid' and 'ninefold' for something surpassing even that. Kyoto (formerly Heiankyo, the 'new capital') is often referred to in classical literature as *kokonoe no miyako*, or 'the nine-layered capital' (a reference to the imposing size of its buildings). *Kokonoe* (literally, 'nine') is translated here as 'nine splendid gates' in reference to the palace of the Chinese emperor, which was said to have nine gates – nine being an auspicious number. The term 'nine-layered' could also be used to refer to the members of the court, in the sense that they themselves had been rendered auspicious by living within a figuratively 'nine-gated' palace. The poem thus pays a compliment to Michinaga and his daughter Shoshi, the then reigning empress.

Ise no Taifu (*fl.* mid eleventh century), not to be confused with the Lady Ise (poem 19), was the granddaughter of Onakatomi no Yoshinobu (poem 49) and a lady-in-waiting to Empress Shoshi (988–1074). Fifty-one poems of hers appear in the imperial *waka* anthologies and she has a private poetry collection. She is one of both the **Thirty-Six Poetic Geniuses of the Late Classical Period** and the **Thirty-Six Women Poetic Geniuses**.

62

This brilliant and witty poem first appeared in *Makura no sōshi* (The Pillow Book; completed 1002), Sei Shonagon's famous collection of miscellaneous musings, and alludes to a well-known story about the Lord of Meng-ch'ang (d. 279 BCE), who escaped through the barrier of Han Ku by imitating the sound of a cock crowing, whereupon the guards, thinking it was dawn, opened the gates.

In Heian romance, the crowing of the cock announces the dawn and the mandatory parting of lovers. Convention ruled that the man must remain with the lady until dawn, but if the man found the lady disagreeable, he would sometimes leave in the middle of the night. In this poem, the poet's lover imitates the sound of a cock crowing and then writes her a note the next day saying that he had wanted to stay longer, but the crowing of the cock had forced him to leave earlier than he wished. The point of the poem is that even though the Chinese guards may have been fooled into opening the Han Ku Barrier, the Osaka Barrier – a famous poetic location, translated here as 'Meeting Hill' (see also the commentary to poem 10 and *utamakura*) – will remain shut, and she will not see him again.

Sei Shonagon (965?–1025?) was the daughter of Moyosuke (poem 42) and great-granddaughter of Fukayabu (poem 36), both famous poets. She was a lady-in-waiting to Empress Teishi (977–1001). Author of the celebrated *Makura no sōshi*, she is considered, with Murasaki Shikibu (poem 57) and Izumi Shikibu (poem 56), one of the greatest of the many outstanding women writers of the Heian period. She has fifteen poems in the official *waka* anthologies and a private poetry collection. She is one of both the **Thirty-Six Poetic Geniuses of the Late Classical Period** and the **Thirty-Six Women Poetic Geniuses**; indeed, it was thought at one time that she could be a possible model for Ono no Komachi (poem 9).

63

The background to poem 63 resembles an episode of a soap opera. Speaking directly to a high-ranking lady was a rare privilege in a society in which even exchanges of letters were usually conducted through intermediaries. Here the poet demands to see his beloved, even if only to tell her that they can never meet again. The two lovers are Fujiwara no Michimasa, a nobleman, and Masako (or Toshi, 1001–22), a daughter of Emperor Sanjo (r. 1011–16), who served as Priestess of the Ise Shrine. Because of Michimasa's reputation as a gallant, Sanjo was opposed to the liaison and forbade Masako from seeing him. As a result, Masako became a nun and died prematurely and Michimasa's wife left him and married another man.

In his *Hachidaishō* (Selection from the First Eight *Waka* Anthologies; 1215–16), Teika places the poem next to one by Narihira (see also poem 17) about his ill-fated encounter with the Priestess of Ise, showing that he understood and appreciated the tragic nature of the liaison that had spawned both poems. The late-Heian critic Fujiwara no Kiyosuke (poem 84), though he did not consider Michimasa to be an exceptional poet, none the less says of this poem: 'When the words perfectly express the thought, naturally a superior poem will result. This is no doubt what is meant by the words "when there is an emotion inside, it will find expression in words"' (*Fukuro zōshi* (Classic of Poetry); 1156–9?).

Fujiwara no Michimasa (992–1054), the son of Minister Korechika, was Master of what is now called West Kyoto (Sakyo no Taifu) until he was removed from power by Michinaga, because of his affair with Princess Masako. From 1016, he led the life of a dilettante recluse. Seven poems of his appear in the imperial *waka* anthologies.

64

Poem 64 describes the Uji River, which runs through an area south of Kyoto where many Heian aristocratic families kept villas and which, as a famous poetic location (see **utamakura**), provides the setting of the famous final chapters of *The Tale of Genji*. The scene is first painted in broad strokes, which then closes in on the fishing nets. The time of the year is winter (indicated by the fishing nets, which were only used in that season) and one can imagine the poet gazing out on the river through the cold mist at dawn.

The poem has been praised for its vivid, straightforward description of the scene, which is completely without human presence. The sound *a* – *Asaborake, araware, ajirogi* – is repeated throughout, giving the poem an airy, liquid quality that perfectly matches the scene being described.

Fujiwara no Sadayori (995–1045) was the eldest son of Kinto (poem 55) and grandson of Emperor Murakami (r. 946–67) on his mother's side. He served as Director for Military Affairs and then as Middle Counsellor. The dedicatee of Koshikibu's poem (no. 60), he was renowned as a poet and calligrapher, with forty-five poems in imperial *waka* anthologies and a private poetry collection. One of the **Thirty-Six Poetic Geniuses of the Late Classical Period**.

65

Wet sleeves are ubiquitous in classical poetry (see also poem 1), but sleeves so wet as to begin to rot are understandably less common. Poem 65 was composed in 1051 for the 'Palace Iris Root Contest of the Fifth Day of the Fifth Month' – so called this because it was held on the same day as a festival for boys, in which iris roots featured. The poem was pitched against the following poem by Minamoto no Takatoshi:

> How I would let you know
> of these flames of grief
> raging beneath,

as a reward for praying
to the Fire-Burning God?

*(Shita moyuru / nageki o dani mo / shirasebaya /
taku hi no kami no / shirushi bakari mo)*

Sagami (b. *c.*1000) is said to be a daughter of Minamoto no Yorimitsu (aka Raiko, 948–1021). The name derives from her husband, Oe no Kin'yori, who was Governor of Sagami (present-day Kanagawa) for some years. She participated in many poetry competitions and established a reputation as a fine poet. Sagami has 110 poems in the imperial *waka* anthologies and a private poetry collection. She is one of both the **Thirty-Six Poetic Geniuses of the Late Classical Period** and the **Thirty-Six Women Poetic Geniuses.**

66

The headnote (*kotobagaki*) to poem 66 as it appears in the *Kin'yōshū* (no. 512) states that it was composed on Mount Omine (a well-known poetic location – see *utamakura*), 'on suddenly seeing a cherry in bloom'. The cherry tree is personified – as it often is in classical Japanese poetry – and asked to feel sympathy for the poet, who has no one else in the world. Gyoson lived for years in the mountains as a mountain hermit.

The phrase *aware to omoe*, translated here as 'let us console each other', literally means to feel compassion for someone or something. The idea of feeling sympathy or pity for a person or thing (*mono no aware*) is an important theme in works of Japanese literature from the Heian period, from the *Kokinshū* to *The Tale of Genji*. Although often associated with the Buddhist idea of impermanence, more generally it describes a basic human concern for the trials and misfortunes of others.

Prelate Gyoson (1055–1135) was the son of Minamoto no Motohira and the grandson of Prince Atsuakira. He entered the Buddhist Onjoji Temple (aka Miidera) in Otsu (in modern-day Shiga Prefecture) and practised the Shugendo austerities of the *Yamabushi* mountain ascetics for many years, eventually becoming head priest of the Tendai sect (in 1123), and Grand Almoner of emperors Shirakawa

(r. 1073–87) and Toba (r. 1107–23). Forty-eight of his poems are included in the imperial *waka* anthologies.

67

The fear of earning a reputation as a fickle person (*adanaru hito*) scared Heian court women at least as much as the fear of being cast off by a lover, but here the point is made in jest. The circumstances that gave rise to poem 67 are described in the headnote (*kotobagaki*) to it in the *Senzaishū* (no. 961): 'On a night of red moon in the Second Month when a number of people had gathered at the Nijo-in to spend the night in conversation, Suo no Naishi lay down and whispered that she wished she had a pillow. Major Counsellor Tadaie heard her, and pressed his arm under the bamboo blind urging her to use it as a pillow.' The word *temakura* (literally, 'arm pillow') is the arm that a lover lays for his partner to rest her head upon. One impressive feature of the poem is how, in so few words, the poet can successfully conjure up the world of Heian-period romance tales. 'Spring', 'night', 'dream' and 'pillow' call to mind young lovers, furtive visits and nights too brief to satisfy the lovers' longing. The phrase *Haru no yo no / yume* (a spring night's dream) is a classical trope for something fleeting and short-lived, incorporating elements of the *yōen* style (see the Introduction, pp. xii–xiii).

Suo no Naishi (d. *c.*1110), given name Nakako, daughter of Taira no Munenaka, Governor of Suo Province, was a handmaid in the inner service (*naishi*) of four emperors, from Emperor Go-Reizei (r. 1045–68) to Emperor Horikawa (r. 1087–1107). She took religious vows in 1108 and died shortly afterwards. Thirty-five of her poems appear in the imperial *waka* anthologies and she has a private poetry collection.

68

Thoughts of leaving the world behind, whether metaphorically or literally, are common in poems from the early eleventh century. The poet here is Retired Emperor Sanjo, and he composed this poem when he was ill and thinking about his abdication. There is a gentle and quiet desperation to poem 68. Rather than bringing comfort, the beauty of the moon only seems to make the sense of dejection more tangible and profound. Sanjo suffered from an eye condition that made him progressively blind. Several misfortunes dotted his reign (the palace burned down twice in two years), and he also suffered from a troubled relationship with the regent, Fujiwara no Michinaga, who eventually forced him to abdicate in favour of his grandson Atsuhira (the future emperor Go-Ichijo, r. 1016–36). There must often have been times when life seemed too much to bear, or when the pain was so acute that dying seemed a better option. Even at such times, however, there is still room in the sovereign's heart to be moved by the beauty of nature.

Retired Emperor Sanjo (976–1017; r. 1011–16), sixty-seventh emperor, was the son of Emperor Reizei (r. 967–9). He became crown prince in 986, but had to wait decades to ascend, only to be forced to abdicate shortly after his enthronement. He was a grandson through his mother of Fujiwara no Kaneie (see commentary to poem 53). Eight of his poems appear in the imperial *waka* anthologies.

69

Poem 69 deftly mixes convention (famous locations, the confusion between maple leaves and brocade) and novel elements to produce a delightful synthesis. Mount Mimuro and the Tatsuta River are both famous poetic locations (see *utamakura*) near the city of Nara in what was once Yamato Province. The Tatsuta River was especially famous as a place for viewing the richly coloured maples in autumn. What makes these traditional elements fresh, however, is the sense of movement within the poem: a mountain gives way to a river, the fury of the storm is followed by the stillness of brocade, all in the space of thirty-one syllables. The poem was composed for a palace poetry contest in 1049 and the gorgeousness of the scenery it evokes perhaps helped it to become the winning poem.

Priest Noin (988–1051?), lay name Tachibana no Nagayasu. After graduating from the imperial university, he entered religion at the age of twenty-five. Noin began his religious life as a peregrinating poet and ascetic and finally settled in Settsu at Kosobe. He is said to have visited many famous sites with poetic associations and is the author of a famous treatise related to this, the *Nōin utamakura*, from the mid Heian period. Sixty-five poems of his appear in the official *waka* anthologies and he has a private poetry collection. He is one of the **Thirty-Six Poetic Geniuses of the Late Classical Period.**

70

According to the standard periodization, the Japanese Middle Ages (*chūsei*) started later than in Europe, at the end of the twelfth century. But poem 70, which dates to the first half of the eleventh century, reflects a decidedly medieval sensibility. Whereas earlier poets expressed in verse the beauty they saw around them, medieval poets sought to create beauty in and through their poetry. In the world of Japanese poetry, autumn is traditionally the season of loneliness and dusk is the most melancholic time of the day, so when one feels listless on the inside, outside it cannot but be an autumn dusk.

Teika's father Shunzei (poem 83) wrote at the beginning of his *Korai fūteishō* (A Treatise on Poetic Styles Through the Ages; 1197–1201): 'If there were no such thing as poetry, people would not understand what scent and colour are, and there would be no way to express the depth of our hearts.' In other words, it is poetry that shapes our perceptions, and gives us a repertoire of images and words to rely on in expressing them.

Priest Ryozen (*fl.* mid eleventh century) was a Tendai monk who became Abbot of Gion Monastery. He lived as a hermit at Ohara and, at the end of his life, at the Unrin'in Temple. Thirty-one of his poems appear in the imperial *waka* anthologies.

71

Though composed on a set topic (*dai*) at a poetry gathering (the topic was 'the autumn wind at a house in the fields'), poem 71 reads very much like a sketch from life. Auditory cues and visual imagery are combined to produce a remarkably vivid description of the autumnal landscape. There is also a temporal dimension to the poem, as the wind first blows through the rice fields and then reaches the reed hut. In the original poem, the presence of the poet in the scene is not obvious, but I have made it more so in the translation ('my reed hut') because placing the speaking voice in the scene creates a more immediate poem in English.

Minamoto no Tsunenobu (1016–97), a renowned poet and musician, was the father of Toshiyori (poem 74). At nearly eighty years of age, he was appointed Governor of Dazaifu, tantamount at the time to banishment. He died there two years later, far from home. Eighty-six of his poems appear in the imperial *waka* anthologies and he has a private poetry collection. He is one of the **Thirty-Six Poetic Geniuses of the Late Classical Period.**

72

Both powerful and witty, poem 72 was originally composed as a reply to this poem by Teika's grandfather, Fujiwara no Toshitada (1073–1123), in the **Kin'yōshū** (no. 468):

> Oh, that I could let you know
> that my heart is like
> the waves of Ariso Bay
> pounding on the shore at night
> driven by the winds of secret longing.

> *(Hito shirenu / omoi Ariso no / urakaze ni /*
> *nami no yoru koso / iwamahoshikere)*

In her reply, the poet retorts that an affair with such a fickle man would no doubt cause her much suffering, hence it is not so much the waves as tears that will make her sleeves wet.

Both poems were composed at a love-letter competition in 1102, when the author of poem 72 was around seventy and Toshitada twenty-nine. Rather than an exchange of actual love letters (*zōtōka*), therefore, the poems would have been an exercise in the conventions of poetic love for the purpose of the competition.

The 'poem pillow' (*utamakura*) 'Takashi shore' refers to a beautiful beach on Osaka Bay. The word Takashi puns on the adjective 'high', indicating the height of the waves. Paired with *oto* (reputation), it means 'famous'. The Takashi shore was not famous for anything in particular, but the name was appealing linguistically because it could be used to form various puns.

Lady Kii (*fl.* mid eleventh century) was a lady-in-waiting to Empress Genshi, consort of Emperor Go-Suzaku (r. 1036–45), then to his eldest daughter, Princess Yushi. Thirty-one poems by her appear in the imperial *waka* anthologies. Her poems are collected in the *Ichinomiya no Kii-shū*.

73

Poem 73 superimposes the mist on the nearby hills and the far-away cherry trees on the high mountain to achieve a kind of pictorial depth. Parallelism (a staple of Chinese-language poetry or *kanshi*) features prominently (the cherries and the mist, the mountain peak and the foothills), while the big caesura at the end of line 3 (*saki ni keri* in the original) emphasizes the division of the poem into two distinct but complementary units. The sentiment expressed is a fairly familiar one. The poet hopes the mist will not rise, as it would obstruct the magnificent view. We know from the headnote (*kotobagaki*) to the poem in the *Goshūishū* (no. 120) that it was composed at a gathering held at the house of Inner Minister Moromichi, so the reference to the glory of the cherries in bloom on the peaks of Takasago was probably intended as a homage to the host. The meaning of *Takasago* is 'sand hills piled high', though the actual location is not clear here, unlike in poem 34.

Oe no Masafusa (1041–1111), known by his title of Acting Middle Counsellor, was from a famous lettered family and a child prodigy in Chinese studies. A favourite and confidant of Retired Emperor Horikawa (r. 1087–1107), he was also a brilliant administrator. He served as Governor of Dazaifu (modern-day Kyushu), following in the footsteps of the revered Sugawara no Michizane (poem 24), and rose to be Director of the Treasury but died soon after this appointment. Masafusa left an important body of work in Chinese and in Japanese; 119 of his poems appear in the imperial *waka* anthologies. His poems are collected in the *Gō no sochi shū*.

74

It is hard to replicate in translation the deliberately inarticulate pathos of poem 74. Whereas earlier poets aspired to a perfect balance between heart and expression, poets from the late Heian period onwards frequently sacrificed balance for complexity and depth. Lovers frequently visited the Hase Temple (known then as Hatsuse Temple and often featuring as a poetic location or *utamakura*), on Mount Hatsuse in present-day Nara Prefecture, to pray to the Bodhisattva of Compassion, Kannon, and that is the background to this poem. Roughly paraphrased, the poem says that the poet has prayed at the temple of the Bodhisattva Kannon ('the Goddess of Mercy') for his lover to become less cruel, and that his prayers have gone unanswered. Much of this, however, is left unsaid in the poem, which, literally translated, reads something like this:

> In vain did I pray to Hatsuse (Kannon)
> but this cruel woman
> rages like its mountain gusts.

Teika, who was an admirer of Toshiyori, wrote of this poem in the *Kindai shūka* (Superior Poems of Our Time; 1209): 'The heart is profound and the words just flow from the heart; it is hard to compose a poem like this even if one tries to imitate it. The form of the poem is truly hard to match.'

Minamoto no Toshiyori (1055–1129) was the son of Tsunenobu (poem 71). He is considered the best poet in the entourage of that renowned connoisseur of poetry, Emperor Horikawa (r. 1087–1107). The compiler of the *Kin'yōshū* and the author of an important poetry treatise, the *Toshiyori zuinō* (Toshiyori's Poetic Essentials; 1113), he engaged in a famous polemic with Mototoshi (poem 75) about 'the new mode' of writing poetry. He has 210 poems in the imperial *waka* anthologies and his poems are collected in the *Sanbokuki kashū*.

75

The context of this poem is explained in the headnote (*kotobagaki*) to it in the *Senzaishū* (no. 1023). The author, Mototoshi, had asked Fujiwara no Tadamichi (poem 76) to appoint his son Lecturer at the Yuima (Vimalakirti) Festival, which was celebrated annually at the family temple, Kofukuji (a well-known poetic location – see *utamakura*). As head of the Fujiwara family, Tadamichi had this prerogative. Tadamichi had initially agreed, and replied quoting a famous poem (later included in the *Shin-kokinshū*, no. 1916) traditionally attributed to Kannon, the Bodhisattva of Compassion, in which the Bodhisattva vows to help all those who place their faith in her:

> Have faith in me,
> I will remain in the world
> and save you as long
> as the mugwort of suffering
> fills the fields of Shimeji.

> *(Nao tanome / Shimejigahara no / sasemogusa /*
> *waga yononaka ni / aramu kagiri wa)*

The word *sasemogusa* (like *sashimogusa* in poem 51) is a variant spelling of the word for *mogusa* or mugwort. The poem could be paraphrased: 'Believe in me: I will always help you for as long as I am alive, just as the mugwort that burns you continues to be grown in the fields of Shimegahara.' It is based on the idea of mugwort, or moxa, being burned for treatment in moxibustion – a painful if therapeutic process – which is explained in the commentary to poem 51. It is thought the poem was originally written in reply to a woman in such straits that she wanted to end her life, the 'mugwort of suffering' being a reference to the pain felt by the young woman in particular and by humankind in general.

Tadamichi's invocation of the poem in his reply to Mototoshi was meant to reassure him that he, like Kannon, would grant Mototoshi's wish for his son. Mototoshi's request was not granted, however. In his poem, Mototoshi alludes to Tadamichi's reply and laments that, though he has had complete faith in him, time has passed and no help has been forthcoming: Tadamichi's promises have proved as

insubstantial as the dew on the mugwort. The image of the dew (*tsuyu*),
a symbol of transience in classical Japanese culture, is reinforced here
by the associative words (*engo*) *chigiri-okishi* (we had promised), based
on the verb *oku*, used to describe dew resting on the grass. The word
aware, meanwhile, like the contemporary Japanese word *aa* or 'ah' in
English, is an exclamation of grief or sad resignation. It is expressed in
the translation in the final exclamation mark.

Fujiwara no Mototoshi (1060–1142), son of Minister Toshiie, was
sole Lieutenant of the Imperial Guard of the Palace Gates when he
entered religion in 1138, aged nearly eighty, changing his name to
Kakushin. A judge of many poetry contests, he was a highly respected
poet and chief representative of the 'old style', in contrast to Toshiyori
(poem 74), who championed the 'new style'. A total of 105 of his
poems are included in the imperial *waka* anthologies and there is a
private collection of his poetry. He is one of the **Thirty-Six Poetic
Geniuses of the Late Classical Period**.

76

This wonderful poem was much admired by its original audience.
The eleventh-century chronicle *Ōkagami* (The Great Mirror) notes
that it was ranked equally with a poem from the *Kokinshū* (no. 409),
traditionally believed to be by Hitomaro (poem 3) and one of the
most famous poems of the *waka* tradition:

> So faintly on Akashi Bay
> as dawn approaches
> my heart is in the boat
> disappearing behind an island
> among the mists.

> *(Honobono to / Akashi no ura no / asagiri ni /
> shimagakure yuku / fune shi zo omou)*

In poem 76, the comparison between waves and clouds per se is not
novel, but by combining it with the image of a boat rowing out to sea,
the poem goes beyond the cliché to conjure up a scene of real fresh-
ness and beauty. This is another example of a 'white on white' poem

(see poem 29), or 'elegant confusion' (*mitate*), with the implied blue of the ocean providing a nice contrast.

Fujiwara no Tadamichi (1097–1164), one-time Prime Minister and Grand Chancellor, who entered religion and was known thereafter as the Hosshoji Buddhist Novice. The son of Grand Chancellor Tadazane, he was the father of Jien (poem 95) and elder brother of Yorinaga (see commentary to poem 77). Tadamichi is one of the principal characters in the *Hōgen monogatari* (The Tale of Hogen; completed *c.*1320) and poem 75 is addressed to him. He was reputed highly as a poet in both Chinese and Japanese and had fifty-eight poems in the imperial *waka* anthologies. He left an anthology of his poems and a collection of Chinese verse (*kanshi*).

77

This is one of the finest of the many love poems in the *One Hundred Poets*: even if we are temporarily parted, the poet declares, the thrust of our passion will reunite us, much like a river that is temporarily divided by an island. The poem was composed for the *Kyūan hyakushu* (One-Hundred-Poem Sequence of the Kyuan Era; 1150–53) and was then included, with revisions, in the **Shikashū**. The earlier version of the poem, from the *Kyūan hyakushu*, reads 'unable to flow on' (*Yuki nayami*) in the first line (second line in the translation below), instead of *Se o hayami* (the force of the rapids), which changes the meaning quite significantly:

> Like rushing water
> unable to flow on,
> we may be parted
> by a rock, but in the end
> we will be one again.

Some commentators consider the original version superior, but the change was probably made by the poet himself at the time the poem was included in the *Shikashū*.

Retired Emperor Sutoku (1119–64; r. 1123–41), seventy-fifth emperor, succeeded his father Emperor Toba (r. 1107–23), but was eventually forced to abdicate in favour of his brother, Konoe. When Konoe died, aged sixteen, Sutoku fomented the Hogen Rebellion (1156) with former Minister of the Left, Yorinaga (later known as 'Yorinaga the Bad' on account of this). He was vanquished and banished to Sanuki in Shikoku. A respected poet himself, he ordered Akisuke (poem 79) to compile the *Shikashū*. He has seventy-eight poems in the imperial *waka* anthologies.

78

Poem 78 alludes to a passage in the 'Suma' chapter of *The Tale of Genji* in which the voices of the plovers at dawn bring comfort to Genji in his solitary awakening. The hero of the tale is here compared to a guard keeping watch over the ancient barrier of Suma (near present-day Kobe), who awakens alone every morning to the sound of the plovers crying.

Teika's father Shunzei (poem 83) was the first to stress the importance to poets of studying *Genji*, considered a monument of court culture. Some of Teika's best-known poems are based on passages from the work, including this variation of poem 78:

> As the road of dreams ends,
> I awake from the journey of sleep
> to hear the lamenting plovers
> coming and going at Suma Barrier –
> the voice of Dawn!

> *(Tabine suru / yumeji wa taenu / Suma no seki /
> kayou chidori no / akatsuki no koe)*

In poem 78, *Awaji* puns upon the place name (a famous poetic location – see *utamakura*) and '[I] will not / cannot meet [you]' in classical Japanese – the reason for the sad keening. An alternative translation could thus read:

> Barrier Guard of Suma,
> how many nights
> have you been wakened
> by lamenting plovers going to and fro
> from the Island Where Lovers Cannot Meet?

The word *kayou* in line 2 of the original Japanese means 'to commute', translated above as 'going to and fro' and more simply as 'returning from' in the main translation.

Minamoto no Kanemasa (*fl.* early twelfth century) belonged to the poetry circle of Retired Emperor Horikawa (r. 1087–1107). He has seven poems in the imperial *waka* anthologies.

79

Poem 79 is another poem celebrating the beauty of the moon, a sight rendered all the more precious because the moon is soon to be hidden by the clouds. The technique of ending the poem with a nominal phrase (*taigendome*) – expressed by the use of a dash – which became especially popular in the medieval period, is used here to render the delight and surprise of suddenly seeing the moon appear through a gap in the clouds. The translation attempts to achieve a similar effect by ending the poem with an exclamation of unexpected pleasure. According to the scholar Shimazu Tadao, the sixteenth-century samurai warlord Hosokawa Yusai wrote a note to Akisuke's poem in which he quoted an old Chinese verse (see *kanshi*) about the moon shining clearly between gaps in the clouds and asserted that poem 79 has the 'grace and elegance of Chinese poetry' (Shimazu, *Hyakunin isshu*, p. 170).

Fujiwara no Akisuke (1090–1155), Master of West Kyoto, was a major figure in the literary world of the twelfth century. In 1144 he received an order from Emperor Sutoku (r. 1123–41) to compile the *Shikashū*, which he completed in 1151. He has eighty-four poems in the imperial *waka* anthologies.

Akisuke's father, Akisue, raised by the wet nurse of Emperor Shirakawa (r. 1073–87), was close to the emperor and wielded authority in the court because of this. A poet himself, Akisue copied a portrait of Hitomaro (poem 3) held in the secret collection of the emperor. He also established the Hitomaro Eigu, a *waka* ceremony in honour of the great poet performed in front of the portrait at Akisue's Rokujoke mansion. He gave the portrait of Hitomaro and his own poetry collection, of great size and value, to Akisuke in what is said to have marked the beginning of the hereditary system of poets of the Rokujoke clan.

Akisuke himself had no power or influence, but became famous as a poet, and he was close to Toshiyori (poem 74). The portrait of Hitomaro was later passed to his son, Kiyosuke (poem 84).

80

This is another 'morning-after poem' (*kinuginu no uta*) in the sensual *yōen* style (see the Introduction, pp. xii–xiv) but of a decidedly different tenor to poem 50. The image of tangled hair indicates that the lovers have spent the night together, but it is also a metaphor for the poet's complex feelings after the encounter. Whereas the lover in poem 50 is radiant with joy and wishes to go on living for ever, the one here worries about her partner's level of commitment and the future of their relationship. Like many *Shin-kokinshū*-period poems, this one features a caesura at the end of the first and third lines of the Japanese (an effect captured by the dashes in lines 3 and 4 of the translation), which give it a measure of complexity and narrative development even in the limited space of a *waka*, enabling it to move from the level of pure description (tangled hair) to the poet's state of mind (tangled emotions). Adding to the complexity is the way in which *nagakaran* ('you will always be true'; literally, 'continuing for a long time') forms an associative word (*engo*) with *kurokami* (black hair) because of the implied length of the hair.

The theme of tangled hair in classical poetry was taken up by modern women poets such as Yosano Akiko (1878–1942) and also used to portray complex emotions, especially love.

Taikenmon-in no Horikawa (*fl.* mid twelfth century) was a lady-in-waiting first to the daughter of Emperor Horikawa (r. 1087–1107) who became Priestess of the Ise Shrine, and then to Taikenmon-in, the consort of Emperor Toba (r. 1107–23). In 1143 she entered religion with her mistress. Sixty-six poems of hers appear in the imperial *waka* anthologies and there is a private collection of her verse. She is one of both the **Thirty-Six Poetic Geniuses of the Late Classical Period** and the **Thirty-Six Women Poetic Geniuses**.

81

In poem 81, startled by the song of the cuckoo, the poet looks out, only to see the lingering moon of the dawn. Heian aristocrats eagerly listened out for the song of the cuckoo, which announced the arrival of summer. Here the joy of hearing the cuckoo is only the prelude to the even greater pleasure of seeing the moon in the summer sky at dawn. The dawn moon is also celebrated in poems 21, 30 and 31.

The interesting thing about this poem is that it links a world of sound to a world of sight. The headnote (*kotobagaki*) to the poem in the *Senzaishū* (no. 161) describes the setting, 'hearing the cuckoo at dawn', but what appeals to the eye is not the cuckoo but the moon of dawn. Though it seems slight in English, the original is a magnificent poem with a wonderful rhythm, and was highly praised in many of the old commentaries.

In *The Tale of the Heike*, Sanesada, the author of this poem, appears in a famous episode that also employs an image of the moon. When the capital was moved from Kyoto to Fukuhara in 1180, the poet went to the palace of his older sister, the Grand Empress Dowager Tashi, and composed a poem about the passing of the former capital:

> Arriving at the old capital,
> the moon shines clearly
> over a wasteland of grasses
> and only the autumn wind
> pierces me to the core.

Fujiwara no Sanesada (1139–91) was the nephew of Shunzei (poem 83) and a cousin of Teika. His career suffered a temporary setback under the Taira clan, but he became Minister of the Left after the clan's demise in 1189. Two years later, already ill, he took the tonsure and died shortly afterwards. Renowned as a musician as well as a poet, he left a diary and a private collection of poems, while seventy-eight of his poems appear in the imperial *waka* anthologies.

82

Although it appears in the 'Love' books of the *Senzaishū* (no. 817), poem 82 works best if read as a lament (*jukkai*) on the sorrows of living. An opposition is set up between the poet's ultimately resilient self and his tears, which are presented as more sensitive and fragile and therefore unable to bear the pain. The key to the poem is the contrast between 'life' and 'tears', and the use of this technique was an orthodox method for appealing to an unsympathetic partner.

Priest Doin (1090–*c*.1179), given name Fujiwara no Atsuyori, reached the fifth rank and the office of Lieutenant of the Imperial Stables of the Left. Famous for being mean, he is a poet about whom many tales are told. He was devoted to poetry, and according to the *Mumyosho* (Anonymous Fragments; completed before 1216), even in old age visited the Sumiyoshi Shrine each month to pray he would become a good poet. Doin entered religion late in life, in 1172. He took part in numerous poetry contests throughout his life and also staged his own. While his private poetry collection has not survived, forty-one poems of his feature in the imperial *waka* anthologies. After he died, Shunzei (poem 83) chose eighteen of his poems for the *Senzaishū*. Doin is said to have appeared to the poet in a dream, expressing his joy, but this only made Shunzei feel sadder, and he added two more of Doin's poems to the collection.

83

Poem 83 subverts the quintessentially medieval idea that one can escape from the sorrows of life by retiring to the quietness of the mountains. Even there, the poet warns us, the deer emits its plaintive cry. There is almost certainly an autobiographical element to the poem, as many of Shunzei's closest acquaintances chose to leave the world behind and lead a life of quiet retreat in the mountains. The most celebrated of all medieval recluses, Kamo no Chomei (1155–1216), also famously concludes the account of his life as a hermit, the *Hōjōki* (An Account of my Ten-foot Hut; 1212), with a confession of his failure to achieve the spiritual goals he had set for himself when he chose the path of seclusion.

This poem, composed in 1140 when Shunzei was twenty-six, was highly regarded by Teika. Composed in the same year that his close friend Saigyo (poem 86) became a monk, at the age of twenty-two, it is said to be influenced by poem 5.

Fujiwara no Shunzei (1114–1204), aka Toshinari, the father of Teika and Master of the Empress Dowager's Palace, was the great poetic arbiter of his time. He entered religion in 1176. A protégé of Emperor Toba (r. 1107–23), he adopted the 'new style' of Toshiyori (poem 74). He was a judge of many poetry competitions, and about two thousand of his judgements on individual poems survive. He compiled the *Senzaishū* and wrote several treatises on poetry, notably the *Korai fūteishō* (A Treatise on Poetic Styles Through the Ages; 1197–1201). He has a private collection of verse and some 450 poems in the imperial *waka* anthologies. Associated with him are the very important aesthetic concepts of *sabi* (loneliness), *yōen* (ethereal beauty) and *yūgen* (mystery and depth), which influenced the development of not only *waka*, but *renga*, **Noh** drama and *haiku* (see the Introduction, pp. xii–xiii). W. B. Yeats was attracted by *yūgen* and it influenced his own attempts at Noh plays. *Sabi* was a major ideal in *renga* poetry and in *haiku*, which derived from *renga*'s opening stanza or *hokku*.

84

This is a deeply personal poem that gently mixes remembrance of the past and hope for the future. If time does heal all wounds, the poet asks, will I look back tomorrow with fondness even on the very unhappy times of today? The answer to the question, however, is not straightforward, as the old pains seem nothing compared to the present ones. Composed when Kiyosuke was in his late fifties or early sixties, the poem may be about the author's disappointments, including a dreadful relationship with his father and the failure of the *Shoku-shikashū* (see below) to be classified officially. It is said to be influenced by a poem by the Chinese poet Bai Juyi in his collected works, *Hakushi monju*, which describes the fading joys of life as one ages and how unlikely it is that the future can recapture the joie de vivre of youth.

Fujiwara no Kiyosuke (1104–77) was one of the early great *waka* poet-scholars of the late Heian period. The second son of Akisuke (poem 79), he is said to have been in conflict with his father until his thirties. As leader of the Rokujo house of poetry founded by his grandfather Akisue (see commentary to poem 79), he took an active part in the literary debates of his time. A rival of Teika, he wrote poetic treatises (*Ōgishō*, *Waka dōmōshō*) and a major compendium of poetic lore, the *Fukuro zōshi* (Classic of Poetry; 1156–9?). In 1165, Emperor Nijo (r. 1158–65) ordered him to compile the sequel to the *Shikashū*, an honour to which every poet aspired, but since the emperor died before its completion, the *Shoku-shikashū* (Later Collection of Verbal Flowers; 1165) was never officially classed as an imperial *waka* anthology.

85

This poem, in the *yōen* style (see the Introduction, pp. xii–xiii), uses highly unusual imagery (the gaps in the sliding door of a bed chamber) to express a familiar concept: the pain of a night spent alone waiting for a lover who does not come. The lover waiting would typically be a woman, so here the poet is adopting a female persona (see *matsu onna*). Though this is a love poem, the reference to persistent darkness calls to mind the Buddhist characterization of the sentient world as a place of darkness, where humans wander waiting to be illuminated by the light of the Buddha, a reading which was no doubt intended by the poet (a Buddhist priest).

This is a poem on an assigned topic (*dai*), but the sentiment of the last two lines is quite unique.

Priest Shun'e (1113–91?), son of Toshiyori (poem 74), was the mentor of Kamo no Chōmei (see commentary to poem 83), who recorded in his *Mumyō shō* (A Nameless Treatise; written from 1211) many of his master's words. Shun'e named his Shirakawa house *Karin'en* (Poem-Wood-Garden), and he often held poetry parties, attended by famous poets. Shun'e himself made several compilations of poems, but he was not as innovative or experimental as his father. In addition to a private collection of verse, eighty-three poems of his appear in the imperial *waka* anthologies. He is one of the **Thirty-Six Poetic Geniuses of the Late Classical Period.**

86

Although this is not one of Saigyo's best-known poems, he seems to have rated it quite highly because he included it in his private poetry collection, the *Sankashū* (Mountain-Hut Anthology; 1180–85?), and in his 'Poetry Contest at the River Mimosuso' (*c.*1187), a fictional contest in which he pitted his best poems against each other with actual judgements on the individual poems provided by Shunzei (poem 83). According to the headnote (*kotobagaki*) to the poem in the *Senzaishū* (no. 926), the poem was composed on the motif 'Love by Moonlight'. The face of the moon here is compared to the face of the beloved: both are disarmingly beautiful and out of the poet's reach. However, the poem is more than just a love poem and can be read more as a general meditation on the human condition. Partly because of its importance in Buddhist discourse, many of Saigyo's finest poems feature the moon, including the following (*Shin-kokinshū* no. 1993), regarded as one of the greatest in classical Japanese literature:

> If my wish were to come true
> I would die in spring
> under cherry blossoms
> of the second month,
> when the moon is full.

> *(Negawaku wa / hana no moto nite /*
> *haru shinamu / sono kisaragi no / mochizuki no koro)*

Saigyo loved flowers too, especially the cherry blossoms of Yoshino, which was also a place of religious significance.

Priest Saigyo (1118–90), lay name Sato Norikiyo, was an officer of the Imperial Guard of the Left. A friend of Shunzei (poem 83), he abandoned his wife and family and entered religion at the age of twenty-two, becoming famous as a wandering poet-monk. Many later travelling poets took him as their model and inspiration, including the great *haiku* master Matsuo Basho (1644–94). The moon, cherry blossoms and solitude were his preferred themes. He edited several private collections of his poems, the most famous being the *Sankashū*. A total of 266 of his poems appear in imperial *waka* anthologies. A legend about Saigyo features in the **Noh** play *Eguchi* by Zeami.

87

The most appealing aspect of poem 87 is the precision and detail with which the landscape is described. The cold rains of autumn have yet to dry when wisps of white fog start to rise, standing out against the dark background of the pine trees. The transition from the small droplets of water on the leaves to the scene as a whole has an almost cinematic quality to it, and calls to mind a camera slowly panning out from a close-up shot. Time is also important as the poem captures the exact moment when the rain gives way to the fog.

The original poem uses a sharp break – *taigendome* – (see also commentary to poem 79), which may be rendered dash on the fourth line, creating a division between the natural scene and the summation by the poet:

> and wisps of fog rise –
> the autumn dusk.

But I have opted for a less dramatic translation, which I believe is closer to the gentle sentiment of the poem.

Priest Jakuren (lay name Fujiwara no Sadanaga, 1139–1202) was the nephew and adopted son of Shunzei (poem 83), and a member of the Mikohidari house of poetry alongside Teika and Ietaka (poem 98). He entered religion in 1192. Appointed a member of the Bureau of Poetry in 1201, he participated in the compilation of *Shin-kokinshū*, but died before it was completed. He has a private poetry collection and 117 poems in the imperial *waka* anthologies.

88

In the original Japanese, poem 88 is perfectly intelligible while containing an astonishing quantity of punning and wordplay. *Karine* means both a 'brief sleep' and 'cut reeds'; *hitoyo* is both 'a single night' and 'one stalk' of a reed; *miotsukushi* (channel marker; rendered *miotsukushite* in the poem), is very similar to the phrase *mi o tsukusu*, which means 'to wear oneself out' (usually with feelings of love), a commonly used pun in love poetry. (See also commentary to poem 22.) Through

punning, two distinct sets of imagery are conflated, one dealing with
the natural setting (cut reeds, a stalk, channel markers) and one with
the imagery of love (brief sleep, a single night, wear oneself out). English simply does not have enough homonyms to create such an effect.
According to the headnote (*kotobagaki*) in the *Senzaishū*, the
poem (no. 807) was composed on the topic 'Love: Encounter at a Traveller's Dwelling'. In Teika's time, the Naniwa Inlet (see *utamakura*)
was a place famous for meeting pleasure girls. Channel markers, frequently referred to in love poetry (see poem 20), were made of wood
and decayed quickly in the salt water. The reeds of Naniwa, a much-
used metaphor for a short time span, also appear in poem 19.

Kokamon-in no Betto (*fl.* late twelfth century), the daughter of
Minamoto no Toshitaka, was lady-in-waiting to Empress Seishi
(1122–81), later known as Kokamon-in. She was a regular attendant
at poetry contests. Only nine of her poems appear in the imperial
waka anthologies.

89

Poem 89 is based on the famous motif of a string of gems (*tama
no o*) – pearls or other jewels such as jade strung together in a necklace or bracelet – which was widely employed in Japanese literature of
the Heian period as a metaphor for life. The word *tama* can mean
both 'pearl ' and 'soul', hence the breaking of the thread of gems
sometimes even symbolized death.

Whereas the previous poem is rife with imagery and wordplay,
poem 89 is quite stark. In the Japanese, the fierce strength of the first
part of the poem contrasts sharply with the quiet, pensive tone of the
last section. The translation reverses the order of the images to have
the more powerful lines come at the end of the poem.

Princess Shokushi (d. 1201), aka Shikishi, a daughter of Emperor Go-
Shirakawa (r. 1155–8), served as Priestess of the Kamo Shrine from
1159 to 1169. She studied poetry under Shunzei (poem 83) and later
under Teika. Tradition has it that it was for her that Shunzei wrote his
treatise *Korai fūteishō* (A Treatise on Poetic Styles Through the Ages;
1197–1201). Although she was much older than him, there is a tradition that she and Teika were lovers, though this is unlikely. She

appears in Zeami's **Noh** play *Teika*. There is a private collection of her verse and she has fifty-five poems in the imperial *waka* anthologies.

90

Poem 90 is both an allusion and a response to a poem composed more than a century earlier by Shigeyuki (poem 48) in the *Goshūishū* (no. 827):

> At Matsushima
> only the fisherfolk
> fishing on the shore of Ojima
> can have sleeves
> as drenched as mine.

> *(Matsushima ya / ōjima no iso ni / asari seshi /*
> *ama no sode koso / kaku wa nureshika)*

Though not stated directly, the sleeves are wet from tears of love. Ojima in the poem is a well-known poetic location (see *utamakura*), used to add resonance.

Poem 90 develops the imagery of the original poem by stating that not only are the poet's sleeves thoroughly soaked, but they have changed colour, presumably because the crying has continued for so long. Some commentators suggest that the sleeves have turned red not out of excessive crying but because the poet has been crying tears of blood, a conventional image in Chinese poetry (*kanshi*) for deep despair – believed to derive from the story of Bian He, who cried tears of blood when wrongfully accused of having presented a fake piece of jade to the King of Chu – but this is not the standard view.

Inpumon-in no Taifu (*c.*1130–*c.*1200), the daughter of Fujiwara no Nobunari, served a daughter of Emperor Go-Shirakawa (r. 1155–8), Princess Ryoshi (known as Inpumon-in). Highly esteemed by Teika (poem 97), she took part in many poetry contests and was a member of the Karin'en poetry circle. There is a private collection of her verse and sixty-three poems by her appear in the imperial *waka* anthologies.

91

Here, lines from old poems are put together almost like pieces of a jigsaw puzzle to create a lovely picture of autumnal melancholia. Among the source poems that contemporary readers would have recognized is a poem from the *Kokinshū* (no. 689):

> Upon the straw mat
> is she spreading out her robe
> and waiting for me
> alone again tonight –
> the Maiden of the Bridge of Uji.

> *(Samushiro ni / koromo katashiki / koyoi mo ya /
> ware o matsuramu / Uji no hashihime)*

They would have also recognized one from the *Shūishū* (no. 778), by Hitomaro, which also appears in this collection as poem 3.

Spreading out a 'robe for one', referred to in both the poem above and poem 91, derives from the practice of lovers spreading out their robes when they slept together (see *kinuginu no uta*). The image of a single robe, rather than two placed companionably together, poignantly conveys the lonely night-time vigil of the poet, waiting in vain for a lover who will never come.

Though clearly a love poem, poem 91 also captures the sadness of autumn, which is why it originally appeared in one of the 'Autumn' books of the *Shin-kokinshū* (no. 518). It was composed in 1200 for a one-hundred-poem sequence commissioned by Emperor Gotoba (poem 99).

Fujiwara no Ryokei (1169–1206), son of Grand Chancellor Kanezane and nephew of Jien (poem 95), became Minister of the Left in 1199, regent in 1200 and chancellor in 1204. He was also a member of the Bureau of Poetry, and took part in the compilation of the *Shin-kokinshū*, for which he also wrote the preface. He has a private collection of verse, while 320 poems of his appear in the imperial *waka* anthologies. He is one of the **Thirty-Six Poetic Geniuses of the Late Classical Period.**

92

When used wisely, convention can be a wonderful means of adding depth and complexity to a new poem. Hidden feelings and wet sleeves are familiar ingredients in *waka*, but poem 92 is effective precisely because it uses these images in an unconventional way. Indeed, the poem was so admired that Sanuki apparently became known as 'Rocks-in-the-offing Sanuki' (Oki no ishi no Sanuki). The lover's sleeves are compared to underwater rocks far away from the shore, always hidden from view, and always wet (from tears). The word *hito* (literally, 'person'; translated here as 'you') can mean either the person that the poem would have been directly addressed to or a third-party observer. Using only age-old expressions, the poem manages to be fresh and interesting, so can be seen as a textbook application of Teika's dictum to combine 'old words but with a new heart' (*kotoba furushiki kokoro atarashiki*).

Lady Sanuki (*c.*1141–1217) was the daughter of Minamoto no Yorimasa, a prominent warrior and poet and one of the main characters in the late-Heian war epics *The Tale of the Heike* and *The Tale of Heiji* (*Heiji monogatari*). She was a lady-in-waiting to Ninshi, the consort of Emperor Gotoba (poem 99). Seventy-three of her poems appear in the imperial *waka* anthologies and she was one of both the **Thirty-Six Poetic Geniuses of the Late Classical Period** and the **Thirty-Six Women Poetic Geniuses**.

93

This is a simple poem about the seascape off the port of Kamakura (a well-known poetic location or *utamakura*), which tells of the poet's wish for the world to remain the same. It acquires extra poignancy when one considers that the author was assassinated in the very same area at the young age of twenty-seven. Like the previous poem, this one also makes use of earlier poems by other poets, including one anonymous poem from the *Kokinshū* (no. 1088):

> In Michinoku everywhere's lovely
> but my heart leaps up

at the sight of boats
pulled by ropes
along the Bay of Shiogama.

*(Michinoku wa / izuku wa aredo / Shiogama no /
urakogu funa no/ tsunade kanashimo)*

Sanetomo is known for his predilection for the archaic style of the
eighth-century **Man'yōshū** as opposed to the more polished style of
later imperial *waka* collections; this can be seen here in his use of
archaic diction in line 2, *tsune ni mogamo na* (also appearing in
Man'yōshū no. 22). The phrase *mogamo na* (how I wish it were like
this) is an old expression not widely used in poetry from the Heian
period onwards.

Minamoto no Sanetomo (1192–1219) was the third Kamakura sho-
gun. He studied poetry from childhood and was taught by Teika
(poem 97). Teika, who was anything but a flatterer, praised Sanetomo
as having surpassed him by the early age of twenty. Teika's *Kindai
shūka* (Superior Poems of Our Time; 1209) is said to have been writ-
ten as a manual for the younger poet's instruction. Though appointed
shogun in 1203, Sanetomo was a virtual prisoner of his family on the
maternal side. He had a tragic destiny and was assassinated by his
nephew Yoshinari in 1219. He was considered with Saigyo (poem 86)
to be among the greatest poets of his day. His poems are collected in
the *Kinkaishū*. A total of ninety-three poems of his appear in the
imperial *waka* anthologies.

94

Poem 94 draws on both Chinese and Japanese literary precedents to
paint a charming picture of autumnal melancholia. The great Tang
poet Li Bai (701–62) wrote four songs of the seasons, one of which,
'Ziye Song', describes the sound of fulling mallets echoing in the
autumn wind. Once washed, clothes were pounded with a mallet on
a wooden block or stone, to dry and soften them and to bring out a
sheen, in a process that was the forerunner of the domestic smoothing
iron. The image was often used to symbolize restoring love gone dull
to its pristine beginnings. A translation of Li Bai's poem might read:

A slip of the moon hangs over the capital.
Ten thousand fulling mallets are pounding,
and the autumn wind is blowing my heart.

The image also appears in 'Early Autumn, Alone at Night' by Bai Juyi (772–846). In the Chinese poetic tradition (see *kanshi*), the sight and sound of a mallet beating cloth on the fulling block reminded a husband far away from home of his distant wife. Burton Watson's translation of this poem reads:

> Parasol tree by the well, cold leaves stirring;
> nearby fulling mallets that speak an autumn sound:
> I sleep alone facing the eaves,
> wake to find moonlight half over the bed.*

Poem 94 also draws directly on one in the *Kokinshū* (no. 325) by Ki no Korenori, which describes Mount Yoshino getting colder as the snow piles up in winter. In poem 94, here the season is autumn and the snow is replaced by the image of cloth being fulled at dusk, resulting in a charming example of synaesthesia (the cold sound of the mallet). *Samuku* (coldly) in line 4 acts as a **pivot word** between *furusato* (old home) and *koromo utsu* (to beat the clothes) to convey the double sense of clothes being beaten in the cold of the evening and the 'chilly' sound of the mallet. The word *furusato* in line 4 can be translated both as 'the old capital' or as 'my old home'. In this poem, it is generally understood to refer to the old capital of Yoshino, a famous poetic location (see *utamakura*).

An analysis of these influences helps to illustrate the complex background of many of the poems and how steeped they are in literary antecedents.

Fujiwara no Masatsune (1170–1221), aka Asukai, founded the Kemari football school of that name. In 1198, Emperor Gotoba (poem 99) summoned him from Kamakura and in 1201 assigned him to the Bureau of Poetry, where he took part in the compilation of the *Shin-kokinshū*. There is a private collection of his verse and 134

---

* From *Po Chü-i: Selected Poems*, translated by Burton Watson. Copyright © 2000 Columbia University Press. Reprinted with permission of Columbia University Press.

poems of his appear in the imperial *waka* anthologies. He is one of the **Thirty-Six Poetic Geniuses of the Late Classical Period.**

95

Poem 95, written when the author was thirty-two, constitutes a vow to devote one's life to the salvation of others. The phrase 'in these wooded hills' (*waga tatsu soma ni*) was used in a poem by the monk Saicho (767–822), the founder of the Japanese Tendai sect of Buddhism, to refer to Mount Hiei, the central temple of the sect and a well-known poetic location (**utamakura**). The word *sumi* in line 5 is a pun (**kakekotoba**) meaning both 'to reside' – on Mount Hiei – and 'to dye' (one's robes black). Though the exact circumstances of composition of the poem are unknown, some scholars speculate that it may have been composed in 1187, when a series of misfortunes hit the area of the capital (as described in the *Hōjōki* of Kamo no Chomei – see commentary to poem 83), causing much despair and leading to a heightened sense of religious mission among the clergy. Teika's father Shunzei (poem 83) remarked of this poem: 'Right from the first line, it is full of heartfelt sentiment, and everything down to the last overtone of the final verse is absolutely charming' (*Jichin Kashō jika-awase* (Tournaments of One's Own Poems); 1198?).

The first line, which could also be translated as 'Though I hesitate to say', expresses the monk's humility before the task ahead.

Former High Prelate Jien (1155–1225) was the son of Grand Chancellor Fujiwara no Tadamichi (poem 76), brother of Kanezane and uncle of Ryokei (poem 91). He entered religion in 1165, at the age of ten, and eventually became Superior General of the Tendai sect in 1192, after serving as Grand Almoner to Emperor Gotoba (poem 99) since 1184. Jien is famous as the author of the *Gukanshō* (A Modest Look at History; 1219), an important work in which he sets out to find the meaning of history from a Buddhist perspective. A member of the Bureau of Poetry, he was also in the circle of Shunzei and of his nephew Ryokei. He penned a private collection of verse and has some 270 poems in the imperial *waka* anthologies. He was one of the **Thirty-Six Poetic Geniuses of the Late Classical Period.**

96

While hinting at the 'elegant confusion' (*mitate*) between blossoms and snow so often used by earlier poets, the first part of this poem has the imagistic richness typical of the *yōjō* (overflowing emotion) style in vogue in the late-Heian and early-Kamakura periods. The verb *furi-yuku* in line 4 is a pun (*kakekotoba*) meaning both 'to fall' and 'to age' and marks the transition from the seasonal sketch in the first section of the poem to personal meditation in the second part. At the age of sixty, Kintsune took the tonsure to study under the famous priest Myoe (1173–1232). In doing so, he left behind the spectacle and glamour of court life. Although the exact date of composition of this poem is unknown, it is likely that it was composed soon after this event as a look back on a lifetime of frantic activity from the perspective of someone who has renounced the world to enter monastic life.

Teika wrote a poem based on this motif in his private collection of poems, the *Shūigusō* (no. 59):

> I have passed the years
> longing for the blossoms,
> lamenting the parting of the moon
> but, gazing at deep snow, I realize
> how my age has piled up too.

> *(Hana o machi / tsuki o oshimu to /sugushite kite /*
> *yuki ni zo tsumoru / toshi wa shirareru)*

Fujiwara no Kintsune (1171–1244) was appointed Chancellor of the Realm in 1222 and then entered religion in 1231. He founded the illustrious Saionji sub-clan of the Fujiwara. His elder sister was Teika's wife. Regarded as one of the best poets of his time, he has a total of 114 poems in the imperial *waka* anthologies.

97

As his only contribution to the *One Hundred Poets*, Teika chose this poem of passionate longing for a lover who never comes. Much of the imagery and wording of the poem comes from a *chōka* in the *Man'yōshū* (no. 935), reflecting Teika's practice of using old diction in new compositions. But whereas the original poem focuses on the hesitations of a traveller who does not have the courage to reach the shore where lovely fisherwomen are at work, here the poem is written from the point of view of a woman (see *matsu onna*), whose smouldering passion is compared to the salt-making fires lighting up the shore at Matsuho Bay (translated here as 'the Bay of Waiting'), a well-known poetic location (see *utamakura*). At the time, brine and seaweed were brought up from the sea in carts and boiled down on the shore to make salt.

Many of Teika's best love poems allude to old romances, both real and literary, but not out of mere admiration for the past. He believed that the timeless, ever-renewing sentiments of love acquired new depth and resonance when superimposed on or paired with the memory of past loves. The poem was composed in 1216 at a palace poetry contest hosted by Emperor Juntoku (r. 1210–21).

Fujiwara no Teika (1162–1241), aka Sadaie, the son of Shunzei (poem 83) served as Acting Middle Counsellor. One of the compilers of the *Shin-kokinshū* and the sole editor of the *Shin-chokusenshū*, for which he also wrote the preface. A poet, scholar, critic and philologist, he collated and produced faithful copies of many important Heian works, ensuring their survival. He is the author of several treatises and collections and kept a diary in Chinese, the *Meigetsuki* (Chronicle of the Bright Moon). As a person, he is said to have been conspicuously ugly and irascible, but was recognized as a great poet and authority on, and judge of, poetry. The compiler of the *One Hundred Poets* (see the Introduction, pp. ix–xiv), he published 465 poems in the imperial *waka* anthologies and has a private collection of his verse, the *Shūigūsō*.

98

This poem alludes to one in the *Goshūishū* (no. 231), which reads:

> In the summer mountains
> oak leaves rustling
> in the summer dusk –

this year, too –
feel like autumn.

*(Natsu yama no / nara no ha soyogu / yūgure wa /
kotoshi mo aki no / kokochi koso sure)*

According to the headnote (***kotobagaki***) to this poem in the ***Shin-
chokusenshū*** (no. 192), it was composed for an ornamental screen (see
the Introduction, p. xxv) made in celebration of the entrance to court
of Shunshi (1209–33), consort of Emperor Go-Shirakawa (r. 1210–21).
Monthly rituals and festivals (known as 'annual observances' or *nenjū
gyōji*) were a common motif for these screens. A different observance
was painted on each panel of the screen, one for each of the twelve
months. The particular scene for which this poem was composed is
the purification ablution (*misogi*) of the sixth month (late summer in
the **lunisolar calendar**); the poet amusingly remarks on the contrast
between the time of the poem he cites (autumn) and the time of the
painting (summer). The Oak Brook, or *Nara no ogawa* (literally, 'Nara
River', but with no connection to the city of Nara in Yamato Province),
is a little stream that runs through the Kamo Shrine in Kyoto. The
word 'Nara' is traditonally written in ***kana*** rather than ***kanji*** because
it has two meanings, one being the name of a tiny shrine within the
grounds of the Kamo Shrine itself and the other being 'oak', as used in
the translation. It is a good example of how *kana* allow for the possibil-
ity of linguistic play, which the translation, 'Oak Brook', endeavours to
convey. The stream was also known as *Mitarashigawa* (literally, 'Water-
Pouring River') because of its role in Shinto purification rituals.

Fujiwara no Ietaka (1158–1237), of the junior second rank, served as
Director of the Ministry of Palace Affairs. He was son-in-law to
Jakuren (poem 87) and studied under Shunzei (poem 83). One of the
compilers of ***Shin-kokinshū***, he was an intimate of Emperor Gotoba
(poem 99) and continued to correspond with him, even after Goto-
ba's banishment. He left a private collection of verse and 280 poems
in the imperial ***waka*** anthologies.

99

This is a poem in the *jukkai* (lament) subgenre, which poets used to
voice their despair at misfortunes ranging from ageing to the death of

a dear one. There are an endless number of interpretations for the last two lines of the poem, which are described in the Note on the Translation, p. xxxviii.

Although highly lyrical and almost certainly at least partly autobiographical, the poem was composed for a one-hundred-poem sequence (*hyakushū*) to which Gotoba contributed in 1201 with Teika, Ietaka (poem 98), Fujiwara no Hideto (1184–1240) and an unknown fifth poet. *Hyakushū* poems were composed on set topics (*dai*), but this does not necessarily mean that they lacked spontaneity or depth; indeed, the challenge was precisely to be able to infuse real emotion and pathos in poems on a set theme.

Mono-omou in the last line usually refers to musings of an amorous nature, but here it means dejected thoughts in a more general sense.

Retired Emperor Gotoba (1180–1239; r. 1184–98), the eighty-second emperor, was the son of Emperor Takakura (r. 1168–80). He was also the younger brother of the child emperor Antoku (r. 1180–85), whom he succeeded at the age of four when the Taira clan took Antoku to the western provinces and drowned him rather than allowing him to be captured by a rival clan. Gotoba abdicated in 1198 but remained de facto sovereign in the names of his sons Tsuchimikado and Juntoku (poem 100). In 1221, he moved against the Kamakura shogunate, but the revolt failed and he was exiled to the Oki Islands (see commentary to poem 11 and **utamakura**), where he spent his last eighteen years. He was deeply interested in poetry, and personally took part in the compilation of the **Shin-kokinshū**. He also started a vogue for **renga**. He left a private collection of verse and a treatise on poetry, the *Gotoba no in gokuden* (The Retired Emperor Gotoba's Secret Teachings). Completed after 1212, Teika and he were at loggerheads frequently but had mutual respect for each other (see the Introduction, p. x).

100

The last poem in the *One Hundred Poets* returns to the theme of imperial power – in this case the loss of it – with which the collection opens but looked at from a decidedly different angle. Whereas Tenji's opening poem implies a benevolent emperor ruling over a people, this one is filled with nostalgia for the past glories of the imperial

house. The main rhetorical device is a **pivot phrase** that also func-
tions as a pun (*kakekotoba*), *nokiba no shinobu* (rendered *noki-ba no
shinobu* in the poem) – which means both the 'memory ferns growing
on the eaves' and 'to remember nostalgically/to long for the past'.

The last lines are the key to the poem: no matter how much we
may long for it, the past is always more glorious than even our fondest
recollections. I have translated the last lines as a personal lyric, but as
the poem is by an emperor, these could also be translated as 'that
glorious reign of old / cannot be brought back'. A more literal trans-
lation would read:

> No matter how I yearn for it,
> my yearning never ends
> for the glorious reign of old.

We know from the headnote (*kotobagaki*) in Juntoku's private collec-
tion of verse that the poem was composed in the autumn of 1216,
when the author was only nineteen years of age. Five years later, in
1221, Juntoku took part in his father Gotoba's unsuccessful attempt
to overthrow the military regime and restore direct imperial rule, and
he was deposed and exiled to Sado Island (a well-known poetic
location – see *utamakura*) as a result. Although the poem was com-
posed several years before these traumatic events, our knowledge of
them seems to lend a strangely prophetic poignancy to the poem.

Retired Emperor Juntoku (1197–1242; r. 1211–21), the eighty-
fourth emperor, was the third son of Emperor Gotoba (poem 99).
After the failed rebellion of 1221, he lived in exile on Sado Island,
where he died twenty-one years later. He studied poetry under Teika
(poem 97) and left a large corpus of writings, notably the *Yakumo
mishō* (August Notes on the Eight Clouds; *c.*1219), which, though
mostly devoted to *waka*, is also one of the first treatises to deal ser-
iously with *renga*. He left a private collection of verse and 159 of his
poems are included in the imperial *waka* anthologies.

Glossary

chōka: A poem of variable length made up of alternating lines of five and seven syllables and ending with a couplet of two seven-syllable lines.

engo (associative words): Clusters of semantically related words may be embedded within a poem and highlighted through punning or another rhetorical device to give supplementary meanings and as a show of verbal artistry intended to surprise and delight the reader. One example is poem 19, where the word *yo* – both a 'node' on a bamboo stalk or reed and 'life', 'the world' – is an associative word for *ashi* (reed). Another example can be found in poem 27, where *wakite* (to spring) is an associative word for *izumi* (spring). Such words assist in creating complex layers of meaning in a poem, fusing the external landscape and internal state of mind into one. In a similar vein, editors of poetry collections (*kashū*) would arrange poems in sequences so that they resonated lexically in some way, creating unified clusters of poems that were originally discrete. We can find such examples in the *One Hundred Poets* – see the Introduction, p. xix.

Gosenshū (*Gosen wakashū*; Later Collection of *Waka* Poems): Usually shortened to *Gosenshū*, this collection, compiled in 951, is the second of the imperially commissioned *waka* anthologies. Compared to the *Kokinshū*, it features more poems by women and a much larger number of poetry exchanges (*zōtōka*). The prose headnotes (*kotobagaki*) are much longer and more elaborate, reflecting the literary preferences of the age.

Goshūishū (*Goshūi wakashū*; Later Collection of *Waka* Gleanings): An imperial *waka* anthology compiled in 1086 by Fujiwara no Michitoshi (1047–99), who also wrote the preface to it.

haiku: Formally, a short poem consisting of seventeen syllables, 5-7-5; see the Introduction, p. xxx.

jokotoba (**preface**): The initial segment of a poem serving as a 'preface' to a word introduced later in the poem, to which it is linked via homophony or metaphor. When the first two or three lines of a poem provide an ornamental opening often focusing on aspects of the landscape the poem is said to be a preface-poem (*joka*) and the first two lines are called a 'preface' (*jokotoba*). Typically, the initial segment is linked to what follows via sound repetition or metaphor. Poem 39 is an example. When the preface is unrelated semantically to the content of the main part of the poem, it gives rise to two distinct layers of meaning within the same short poem. A textbook example appears in the third poem of Episode 23 of *The Tales of Ise*:

> As the wild winds blow
> and the white waves rise,
> I think of you
> crossing Mount Tatsuta
> all alone by night.

> (*Kaze fukeba / oki tsu shiranami / Tatsuta-yama /
> yowa ni ya kimi ga / hitori koyuran*)

The first two lines, 'As the wild winds blow / and the white waves rise', serve as a preface for *tatsu* (to rise), which is also the first part of the word of 'Tatsuta' as it appears in *Tatsuta-yama* or Mount Tatsuta.

kakekotoba (**literary pun**): Variously defined in dictionaries of classical Japanese poetry, this term is most commonly taken to mean a form of punning, but whereas a straightforward pun – equivalent to the word *dajare* in modern Japanese – might be viewed as light-hearted and comical and a rather low-grade form of verbal play, the *kakekotoba* in classical Japanese poetry was used to display the highest level of verbal and poetic artistry. That said, there are cases where the punning can be quite humorous, light or even mildly bawdy.

The device does function primarily as a pun, but one that may operate on many levels. Though sometimes the pun can be conveyed by a single word, in many cases it can apply to several lines, so that a string of words or phrases may be punned together. Thus it is possible for several lines of a *waka* poem to give two completely different readings, one that provides the basic message of the poet and the other a form of highly refined verbal decoration often depicting a visual image. This second reading might be related to the main message or it might be a separate pun, or series of puns, with a purely decorative function. The intention was to create a multi-layered effect of great complexity in order to convey the depth of the poet's emotion in a refined and artistic manner. The Japanese language has many homophones and similar-sounding words, which makes such complicated punning possible – wordplay of a kind that would be extremely difficult to simulate in English – and Heian poets deployed the *kakekotoba* to full effect in their verse. A classic example is poem 16, with the pun *matsu* (to wait for someone) and *matsu* (pine tree), which, as it happens, is also one of the rare puns that happens to work perfectly in English.

Translated literally, *kakekotoba* means 'overlapping of words' – effectively punning – but most non-Japanese scholars of classical Japanese studiously avoid using 'pun' as a translation, mostly because of the traditional view of the pun as being low-class. The standard English translation of the term to date is **pivot word/phrase**, which refers more specifically to when a word may be read as the continuation of what precedes it or as the beginning of what follows, producing two different readings. This translation is problematic, however, because *kakekotoba* is mostly defined in Japanese dictionaries with little or no reference to its function as a pivot word. By contrast, Japanese scholars recognize so called 'pivot words' as *kakekotoba* only when they also happen to function simultaneously as puns, tending to see the pivoting function more in relation to other rhetorical devices, such as prefaces (*jokotoba*) and associative words (*engo*), that may be at work in a poem.

In poem 16, *matsu* ('to pine' and 'pine tree') is an example of a pivot word working in tandem with the preface and also as a pun. In poems 27 and 51, the words *Izumigawa* (Izumi River) and *sashimo gusa* (moxa) function as pivot words in tandem with the preface, although they are not puns semantically. Nevertheless, there is kind of aural punning at play: in poem 27, the sound of *Izumi* is echoed later in *itsu mi*, and in poem 51 the sound of *sashimo* is repeated too. A slightly different kind of verbal play occurs in poem 58, whereby the words *kaze fukeba* (literally, 'when the wind blows'; 'the wind whispers' in the translation) lead on to *soyo* (literally, 'I told you so'; 'I swear of my love' in the translation) and onomatopoeically echoes the sound the wind makes.

I have chosen to use 'pun' as a translation for *kakekotoba* with the Japanese in brackets after it, but another option would be not to translate the word at all as in the case, for example, of *waka*, *haiku*, etc. It is an extremely complex term with a wide variety of variations in usage over a long period of time. It should be noted, too, that many of the terms used to describe rhetorical devices were not coined until the Meiji period (1868–1912) and then applied to classical *waka* poetry, which do not always fit neatly within the definitions given to them.

kana and *kanji* (Chinese characters) comprise the Japanese writing system. *Kana* are syllabic Japanese scripts in contrast to logographic Chinese characters. Originally invented for writing Japanese words in particular, each *kana* character corresponds to one sound in the Japanese language. Because of the enormous number of homonyms in Japanese, the creation of *kana* greatly facilitated the development of *waka* poetry, especially **kakekotoba**. A word written in a Chinese character allows for only one meaning, whereas using *kana* enables a word to be read with all its homonyms. For example, the word for pine tree, *matsu*, also means 'to wait' or 'pine for', a multi-layered sense that can be conveyed by *kana* but not by *kanji*. Where *kana* are especially useful are in cases where the written form is the same but the pronunciation of the words differs. A good example is poem 27, where the first part of *Izumigawa* (Izumi River) puns with *itsu mi ka* (literally, 'when will I see you?') as *zu* and *tsu* would have been written in the same way in the Heian period. (See commentary to poem 27 for more on this.)

kanji: See previous entry.

kanshi (**poetry in Chinese**): Poetry written in the Chinese language was called *kanshi* or *karauta*, in contrast to *yamato uta* (poetry of Yamato, Japanese poetry). Chinese learning and literature enjoyed enormous prestige in the early period and account for the majority of the writing by Japanese authors in the eighth and ninth centuries. Chinese poetry also had a profound influence on Japanese poetry, especially at the level of themes and imagery. See poems 23, 29, 31, 36, 73, 79 and 94.

kinuginu no uta (**'morning-after' poem**): Custom demanded that courtiers send a poem to their beloved after a night spent in their company – known as a 'morning-after' poem. These were typically meant to reassure the lady that the lover remained true to his beloved after a night together. The word *kinuginu* is the plural of the word for clothes, *kinu*. Courtiers of the time used the clothes they wore during the day as bedding at night; a couple would use their combined clothing. In the morning, they put on their clothes again before parting, leading to the phrase *kinuginu no wakare*, to describe their parting (*wakare*) in the morning, and the poem (*uta*) that expressed their grief at parting as *kinuginu no uta*. Examples include poems 43 and 50.

Kin'yōshū (*Kin'yō wakashū*; **Collection of Golden Leaves**): An imperial *waka* anthology compiled in 1124–7 by Toshiyori (poem 74) at the command of the Retired Emperor Shirakawa (r. 1073–87). Although the two first versions were rejected by the emperor, the second version, completed in 1126, was widely circulated and became popular among the literary figures of the day. The third version, completed in 1127, received imperial approval, but the emperor kept it to himself and it was not circulated further, as a result of which the second version is still regarded as the standard one.

Kokinshū (*Kokin wakashū*; **Collection of *Waka* Ancient and Modern**): This was the first imperially ordered *waka* anthology of native poetry in Japan. In 905 Emperor Daigo gave the order for its compilation to the poets Tomonori (poem 33), Tsurayuki (poem 35), who was the principal author, Mitsune (poem 29) and Tadamine (poem 30). Many of the poems in the *One Hundred Poets* were either culled from the *Kokinshū* or else heavily influenced by it. See, for example, poems 5, 7, 8, 10, 12, 26, 30, 35, 37, 42, 91, 93 and 94.

kotobagaki (**headnote**): When poems were anthologized, they were often accompanied by a prose headnote (*kotobagaki*) that explained the circumstances of composition. Poems about which nothing was known were simply given the headnote 'topic unknown' (*dai shirazu*). Many headnotes limit themselves to stating the topic and occasion of composition, but some provide long, detailed accounts, sometimes incorporating fictional elements. A significant characteristic of the *One Hundred Poets* (and of similar selections of poems) is that the headnotes that originally accompanied the poems in the source texts are omitted. This may be because the poems were meant to be appreciated as they were, without background information, or because most readers were expected to already know the context of composition.

lunisolar calendar: The ancient Japanese imported from China a modified lunar (lunisolar) calendar consisting of twelve months of twenty-nine or thirty days. As in the Gregorian calendar, each season consisted of three months, though the New Year began in what would be February, roughly a month to a month and a half later than the Gregorian calendar. The twelve-month sequence is as follows: (1) New Year; (2) mid spring; (3) late spring; (4) early summer; (5) midsummer; (6) late summer; (7) early autumn; (8) mid autumn; (9) late autumn; (10) early winter; (11) midwinter; (12) late winter.

makura kotoba **(pillow words):** These are epithets used in conjunction with certain words as conventional embellishments, forming a 'pillow' for the word in question. Used for their sound, meaning or associations, they gave poets a way to add resonance and heighten the rhetorical effect of their poems. Examples include *chihayaburu* (raging) for *kami* (the gods) and *hisakata no* (used of the sky above) for *sora* (sky), *kumo* (clouds) and *tsuki* (moon). The meaning of many of the most ancient pillow words has been lost or is unclear (such as *hisakata no* above or *ashibiki*, used in tandem with 'mountain' or 'mountain bird'), making their translation problematic. Many 'newer' words were created in the time of the eighth-century *Man'yōshū*, but they are less obscure because their connection with the words they introduce – sound repetition or metaphor – is more obvious. Though particularly common in poems of the *Man'yōshū* and other early writings, pillow words continued to be used throughout *waka's* long history for their archaic resonance. The link between the pillow word and the noun they modify can be phonetic (sound repetition), metaphorical or purely conventional. See poems 17 and 33 for examples of poems that make use of pillow words.

Man'yōshū **(Collection of Ten Thousand Leaves):** This is the earliest-surviving collection of Japanese poetry. While the earliest poems go back to at least the early sixth century, the last datable poem was composed in 759 and the editing was completed in *c*.770. It is believed to have been compiled over many decades by numerous people, although the details of the process remain uncertain. The final collection of twenty volumes and over 4,500 poems is believed to have been compiled by the poet Yakamochi (poem 6). Several poems in the *One Hundred Poets* were taken from, or are based on, poems in the *Man'yōshū*.

matsu onna (**waiting woman**): Poems about waiting for a (male) lover were known as 'waiting woman' (*matsu onna*) poems. The motif first became established in China during the Six Dynasties (222–589), and later became a prominent motif in *waka* too. Men also composed poems on this motif by posing as a woman, as in poems 21 and 85. Indeed, it was not uncommon for a man to adopt the persona of a woman when composing a poem.

mitate (**elegant confusion**): Deliberately mistaking one thing for another (frost for blossoms, dew for gems, etc.) was considered extremely elegant and thus it was a frequently used poetic device in poetry of the Heian period. While the device is applied to classical Japanese poetry, the term *mitate* was not coined until the early-modern period. See poem 31, for example, in which the poet confuses the glow of the snow for the moonlight of the dawn. See also poems 29 and 96.

Noh: A major form of Japanese musical drama, Noh has been performed since the fourteenth century, and is still regularly performed today. Traditionally, a Noh programme includes five plays with comic interludes (*kyōgen*); an *okina* Noh play, usually celebratory and centred on a venerable old man, may be presented in the very beginning, especially at New Year and other special occasions. Noh plays may be based on classic works of literature, such as the *Kokinshū*, *The Tales of Ise* and *The Tale of Genji*. Much of the pleasure of the plays derives from the poetic language sung in a rhythmic style and the many literary allusions. Zeami Motokiyo (c. 1363–c.1443) was the foremost writer of Noh plays and the one who brought the form to its artistic peak. He is also famous for his numerous theoretical works on Noh and its performance. Scholars attribute some fifty plays to him.

pivot word/phrase: A word or phrase that acts as a pivot, meaning that it can be read as the continuation of what precedes it or as the beginning of what follows. See the commentary for poems 3, 9, 18, 19, 27, 46, 48, 94 and 100. It can also function as a pun (see *kakekotoba*).

renga: Linked verse; see the Introduction, p. xiv.

sedōka: A poem consisting of two three-line stanzas each consisting of a pattern of 5-7-7 syllables. See also the Introduction, p. xv.

Senzaishū (*Senzai wakashū*; **Collection of a Thousand Years**): An imperial *waka* anthology first compiled in 1187 by Teika's father Shunzei (poem 83) and revised and completed the following year.

Shikashū (*Shika wakashū*; **Collection of Verbal Flowers**): The sixth imperial *waka* anthology, compiled in 1151 by Akisuke (poem 79).

Shin-chokusenshū (*Shin-chokusen wakashū*; **New Imperial Waka Collection**): An imperial *waka* anthology, compiled in 1235 by Teika, who also wrote the preface.

Shin-kokinshū (*Shin-kokin wakashū*; **New Collection of Waka Ancient and Modern**): The eighth imperial *waka* anthology, compiled by six members of the Bureau of Poetry: Teika, Ietaka (poem 98), Jakuren (poem 87), Masatsune (poem 94), Fujiwara no Ariie (1155–1216) and Minamoto no Michitomo (1171–1237). It was initially presented to the emperor in 1205 but not completed until 1210. The Retired Emperor Gotoba (poem 99), who commissioned the volume, edited and re-edited it himself during the period of his exile. Both the emperor's version and the earlier version of 1210 still exist, though the latter is regarded as the standard one.

Shūishū (*Shūi wakashū*; **Collection of Waka Gleanings**): The third of the official *waka* anthologies, compiled in 1005–11; Kinto (poem 55) was involved in editing it.

Six Poetic Geniuses (*Rokkasen*): The six poets named by Tsurayuki (poem 35) in the preface to the *Kokinshū* as the great poets of the early Heian period, a group that later became known as the Six Poetic Geniuses. All six of them have poems in the *Kokinshū*, and all but one, Otomo Kuronushi, have poems in the *One Hundred Poets*. These include Kisen (poem 8), Ono no Komachi (poem 9), Henjo (poem 12), Narihira (poem 17) and Yasuhide (poem 22). In time, this list was superseded by later groupings, including the **Thirty-Six Poetic Geniuses**.

The Tale of Genji (*Genji monogatari*): Written in the early years of the eleventh century at the height of the Heian period, this is the most famous novel in Japanese literature. The author was Murasaki Shikibu (poem 57), a noblewoman and lady-in-waiting, who beautifully depicts the lifestyle of the courtiers of her day. The novel focuses on the romantic life of its central character, Hikaru Genji or 'Shining Genji', while shedding a fascinating light on the customs and mores of aristocratic society of the time. In chapter 2, for instance, the hero and his male friends discuss women and marriage in an exchange that can be thought of as a sort of Heian man's guide to dating and courtship. *The Tale of Genji* was required reading for all those who considered themselves poets, and Teika's father Shunzei (poem 83) was the first to stress the importance of studying it for poets. Some of Teika's best-known poems are based on passages from *Genji*, and one can feel its influence in many poems in the *One Hundred Poets* (see, for example, poems 8, 12, 35, 41, 57, 64, 66 and 78).

The Tale of the Heike (*Heike monogatari*): One of the great classics of medieval Japanese literature, *The Tale of the Heike*, written some time before 1330, is an epic account of the struggle between the Taira and Minamoto clans for control of Japan at the end of the twelfth century. The main theme of the story is the Buddhist law of impermanence, especially the fleeting nature of fortune, illustrated by the fall of the powerful Taira clan. The work is a compilation of many versions passed down orally by *biwa*-playing bards known as *biwa hōshi* or 'lutenist priests'. *The Tale of the Heike* has greatly influenced Japanese culture over the centuries, from **Noh** plays to woodblock prints, and is frequently referenced in modern works.

The Tales of Ise (*Ise monogatari*): Along with **The Tale of Genji** and the **Kokinshū**, *The Tales of Ise* is one of the three most important works in classical Japanese literature and knowledge of it is a prerequisite for understanding Japanese cultural and literary history. Primarily read as poem tales (*uta monagatari*), the work comprises 125 short narratives that function as suitable contexts for the mostly love poems, many of which depict the famous real-life poet, Ariwara no Narihira (poem 17). The aggregate of the diverse episodes creates a unified perspective of the cultural mores, aesthetics and the Way of Love of early-Heian aristocratic society. The work became a basic text in the *education sentimentale* of the Japanese and a fundamental part of the literary education for poets and men and women of learning for a thousand years. It has influenced *waka*, **Noh**, fiction, diaries and all aspects of literature and art since it was written.

The Tales of Yamato (*Yamato monogatari*): This loosely structured collection of tales of aristocratic life, compiled around 951, comprises vignettes of poets, including several from the *One Hundred Poets*,

providing a record of court life in the early decades of the tenth
century.

tanka: A poem (*waka*) of thirty-one syllables arranged in five lines in
an alternating pattern of five and seven syllables; see the
Introduction, p. xv.

Thirty-Six Poetic Geniuses (*Sanjūrokkasen*): Fujiwara no Kinto
(poem 55) compiled an anthology called the *Sanjūrokuninsen*
(Selection of Thirty-Six Poets) in 1009–12, choosing the best
poems of thirty-six poets. The collection was extremely popular
and the poets later became known as the *Sanjūrokkasen* or Thirty-
Six Poetic Geniuses (literally, 'poets of unworldly greatness'), the
first of many similar series of 'thirty-six'. A more accurate translation
would be the 'thirty-six immortals of poetry', though over the
centuries some have proved less 'immortal' than others.

Kinto's idea was much copied, leading to a plethora of selections
of thirty-six poets. Two of the most famous are Fujiwara no
Norikane's (1107–65) *Gorokurokusen* (literally, 'six multiplied by
six'), of whom the poets were known as the *Chūko Sanjūrokkasen*
(Thirty-Six Poetic Geniuses of the Late Classical Period), and the
Nyōbō Sanjūrokunin uta-awase (Poetry Tournament of Thirty-Six
Women Poets), compiled in the Kamakura period, of whom the
poets were known as the *Nyōbō Sanjūrokkasen* (Thirty-Six Women
Poetic Geniuses). The poets in these various series were widely
depicted in Japanese painting and later woodblock prints. And the
number thirty-six became a magical formula in Japanese culture,
used in endless ways all the way down to the Meiji period, one of the
most celebrated examples being Hokusai's *Thirty-Six Views of Mount
Fuji* (*c.*1830–32). (Poem 4 inspired one of Hokusai's prints – see
commentary to that poem. See also **Six Poetic Geniuses**.)

**Thirty-Six Poetic Geniuses of the Late Classical Period (*Chūko
Sanjūrokkasen*):** See previous entry.

Thirty-Six Women Poetic Geniuses (*Nyōbō Sanjūrokkasen*): See
Thirty-Six Poetic Geniuses.

utamakura (place names; literally, 'poem pillows'): A rhetorical
device whereby famous locations were used in poetry for their rich
cultural associations. For example, Mount Yoshino, near Nara, was
connected with deep snow, Sumiyoshi was associated with pines
and the Sumiyoshi deity, and so forth. During the Heian period,
the term *utamakura* seems to have referred to poetic diction in

general, but from the late Heian period onwards it came to refer specifically to place names. Among the famous places mentioned in *One Hundred Poets* are Mount Kagu (poem 2), Tago Bay (poem 4), the Kasuga Shrine (poem 7), Uji (poems 8 and 64), the Osaka Barrier (poems 10, 25 and 62), Mount Tsukuba (poem 13), the Tatsuta River (poems 17 and 69), Sumiyoshi Bay (poem 18), Naniwa (poems 19, 20 and 88), Mount Ogura (poem 26), Yoshino (poems 31 and 94), Ama no Hashidate (poem 60), Mount Mimuro (poem 69) and Awaji Island (poem 78), to name but a few. Their main associations are explained in the annotations to the poems in question while the maps on pp. 244–5 show their actual location.

waka: Poems of thirty-one syllables arranged in five lines in an alternating pattern of 5-7-5-7-7 syllables. The word *waka* also serves as a general term for classical Japanese poetry in all its forms, except *renga* (linked verse) and *haiku*, as opposed to foreign verse, especially Chinese poetry. *Waka* poetry has influenced all aspects of Japanese traditional culture from aesthetics to literature, from **Noh** to the tea ceremony, and scenes from *waka* poems have been widely depicted in art.

From the **Kokinshū** (905) onwards, twenty-one imperial *waka* anthologies (*chokusenshū*) were officially commissioned and selections of poems by most of the poets in the *One Hundred Poets* were included in them. See also the Introduction (p. xi) and **Gosenshū**, **Goshūishū**, **Kin'yōshū**, **Senzaishū**, **Shikashū**, **Shin-chokusenshū**, **Shin-kokinshū** and **Shūishū**. These were in contrast to the private anthologies that the individual poets compiled themselves.

zōtōka (**poetic exchanges**): Exchanges of poems (usually via letters) were known as *zōtōka* (literally, message and reply poems). In the Heian world, romances began with *zōtōka*, so it was essential to be able to compose poetry. As lovers would often not actually see each other until the night that they made love for the first time, they formed impressions of each other based on the poems, the calligraphy and the paper on which they were written, which was often of exquisite design. It was mandatory to send replies to poems received, as the exchange of poems was an essential component of etiquette, and members of the nobility spent time honing their poetic skills. Exchanges of poems could go back and forth any number of times. Some of the poems in the *One Hundred Poets* were originally part of such poetic exchanges but they were included in the collection individually, without context. Recontextualizing existing poems in new poetry collections was common practice and readers who were already familiar with the poems enjoyed appreciating them in new settings. See poem 62. By contrast 'solo' compositions in which poets described their feelings without a specific audience in mind are known as *dokueika* and were read to oneself.

Romanized Transliterations
of the Poems

In the transliterations below, romanization follows the Hepburn system. Only proper nouns are capitalized and the word at the beginning of each poem. Any inconsistencies in spelling between a word as it is glossed in the Commentary and as it appears in a transliteration are due to a different form of the word being used. The words *miotsukushi* and *mi o tsukusu* appear in the annotation to poem 20, for instance, while *mi-o-tsukushite* features in the transliteration of the poem. This is because *miotsukushi* is a noun while *mi o tsukusu* and *mi-o-tsukushite* are differing forms of the same verb, the infinitive and an inflected form. In the Commentary, the infinitive form of a verb is usually given. Differences are generally noted in the Commentary to make it easier for the reader to find the relevant word in the transliteration.

1
Aki no ta no
kari-o no io no
toma o arami
waga koromode wa
tsuyu ni nuretsutsu

2
Haru sugite
natsu kinikerashi
shirotae no
koromo hosu chō
ama no Kaguyama

3
Ashibiki no
yamadori no o no
shidario no
naganagashi yo o
hitori kamo nen

4
Tago no ura ni
uchiidete mireba
shirotae no
fuji no takane ni
yuki wa furitsutsu

5
Okuyama ni
momiji fumiwake
naku shika no
koe kiku toki zo
aki wa kanashiki

6
Kasasagi no
wataseru hashi ni
oku shimo no
shiroki o mireba
yo zo fukenikeru

7
Ama no hara
furisake mireba
Kasuga naru
Mikasa no yama ni
ideshi tsuki kamo

8
Waga io wa
miyako no tatsumi
shika zo sumu

yo o Ujiyama to
hito wa iu nari

9
Hana no iro wa
utsurinikerina
itazurani
waga mi yo ni furu
nagame seshi ma ni

10
Kore ya kono
yuku mo kaeru mo
wakarete wa
shiru mo shiranu mo
Ōsaka no seki

11
Wata no hara
yaso shima kakete
kogiidenu to
hito ni wa tsugeyo
ama no tsuribune

12
Ama tsu kaze
kumo no kayoiji
fukitojiyo
otome no sugata
shibashi todomen

13
Tsukubane no
mine yori otsuru
Minanogawa
koi zo tsumorite
fuchi to narinuru

14
Michinoku no
shinobu mojizuri
tare yue ni
midaresomenishi
ware naranakuni

15
Kimi ga tame
haru no no ni idete
wakana tsumu
waga koromode ni
yuki wa furitsutsu

16
Tachiwakare
Inaba no yama no
mine ni ouru
matsu to shi kikaba
ima kaerikon

17
Chihayaburu
kamiyo mo kikazu
Tatsutagawa
karakurenai ni
mizu kukuru to wa

18
Suminoe no
kishi ni yoru nami
yoru sae ya
yume no kayoiji
hitome yokuran

19
Naniwagata
mijikaki ashi no
fushi no ma mo

awade kono yo o
sugushiteyo to ya

20
Wabinureba
ima hata onaji
Naniwa naru
mi-o-tsukushite mo
awan to zo omou

21
Ima kon to
iishi bakari ni
nagatsuki no
ariake no tsuki o
machiidetsurukana

22
Fukukarani
aki no kusaki no
shiorureba
mube yamakaze o
arashi to iuran

23
Tsuki mireba
chiji ni mono koso
kanashikere
waga mi hitotsu no
aki ni wa aranedo

24
Kono tabi wa
nusa mo toriaezu
Tamukeyama
momiji no nishiki
kami no manimani

25
Na ni shi owaba
Ōsakayama no
sanekazura
hito ni shirarede
kuru yoshi mogana

26
Ogurayama
mine no momijiba
kokoro araba
ima hitotabi no
miyuki matanan

27
Mika no hara
wakite nagaruru
Izumigawa
itsu miki tote ka
koishikaruran

28
Yamazato wa
fuyu zo sabishisa
masarikeru
hitome mo kusa mo
karenu to omoeba

29
Kokoroate ni
oraba ya oran
hatsushimo no
okimadowaseru
shiragiku no hana

30
Ariake no
tsurenaku mieshi
wakare yori

akatsuki bakari
uki mono wa nashi

31
Asaborake
ariake no tsuki to
miru made ni
Yoshino no sato ni
fureru shirayuki

32
Yamagawa ni
kaze no kaketaru
shigarami wa
nagare mo aenu
momiji narikeri

33
Hisakata no
hikari nodokeki
haru no hi ni
shizukokoro naku
hana no chiruran

34
Tare o ka mo
shiru hito ni sen
takasago no
matsu mo mukashi no
tomo naranakuni

35
Hito wa isa
kokoro mo shirazu
furusato wa
hana zo mukashi no
ka ni nioikeru

36
Natsu no yo wa
mada yoi nagara
akenuru o
kumo no izuko ni
tsuki yadoruran

37
Shiratsuyu ni
kaze no fukishiku
aki no no wa
tsuranukitomenu
tama zo chirikeru

38
Wasuraruru
mi o ba omowazu
chikaiteshi
hito no inochi no
oshiku mo aru kana

39
Asajiu no
Ono no shinohara
shinoburedo
amarite nado ka
hito no koishiki

40
Shinoburedo
iro ni idenikeri
waga koi wa
mono ya omou to
hito no tou made

41
Koi su chō
waga na wa madaki
tachinikeri

hito shirezu koso
omoisomeshika

42
Chigirikina
katami ni sode o
shiboritsutsu
Sue-no-matsuyama
nami kosaji to wa

43
Aimite no
nochi no kokoro ni
kurabureba
mukashi wa mono o
omowazarikeri

44
Au koto no
taete shi naku wa
nakanakani
hito o mo mi o mo
uramizaramashi

45
Aware to mo
iubeki hito wa
omōede
mi no itazurani
narinubeki kana

46
Yura no to o
wataru funabito
kaji o tae
yukue mo shiranu
koi no michi kana

47
Yaemugura
shigereru yado no
sabishiki ni
hito koso miene
aki wa kinikeri

48
Kaze o itami
iwa utsu nami no
onore nomi
kudakete mono o
omou koro kana

49
Mikakimori
eji no taku hi no
yoru wa moe
hiru wa kietsutsu
mono o koso omoe

50
Kimi ga tame
oshikarazarishi
inochi sae
nagaku mogana to
omoikeru kana

51
Kaku to dani
e yawa Ibuki no
sashimogusa
sashimo shiraji na
moyuru omoi o

52
Akenureba
kururu mono to wa
shirinagara

nao urameshiki
asaborake kana

53
Nagekitsutsu
hitori nuru yo no
akuru ma wa
ikani hisashiki
mono to ka wa shiru

54
Wasureji no
yukusue made wa
katakereba
kyō o kagiri no
inochi to mogana

55
Taki no oto wa
taete hisashiku
narinuredo
na koso nagarete
nao kikoekere

56
Arazaran
kono yo no hoka no
omoiide ni
ima hitotabi no
au koto mogana

57
Meguri-aite
mishi ya sore tomo
wakanu ma ni
kumogakurenishi
yowa no tsuki kana

58
Arimayama
Ina no sasahara
kaze fukeba
ide soyo hito o
wasure ya wa suru

59
Yasurawade
nenamashi mono o
sayo fukete
katabuku made no
tsuki o mishi kana

60
Ōeyama
Ikuno no michi no
tōkereba
mada fumi mo mizu
Ama no Hashidate

61
Inishie no
Nara no miyako no
yaezakura
kyō kokonoe ni
nioinuru kana

62
Yo o komete
tori no sorane wa
hakaru tomo
yo ni Ōsaka no
seki wa yurusaji

63
Ima wa tada
omoitaenan
to bakari o

hitozute narade
iu yoshi mogana

64
Asaborake
Uji no kawagiri
taedaeni
arawarewataru
se-ze no ajirogi

65
Uramiwabi
hosanu sode dani
aru mono o
koi ni kuchinan
na koso oshikere

66
Morotomoni
aware to omoe
yamazakura
hana yori hoka ni
shiru hito mo nashi

67
Haru no yo no
yume bakari naru
tamakura ni
kainaku tatan
na koso oshikere

68
Kokoro ni mo
arade ukiyo ni
nagaraeba
koishiharuboki
yowa no tsuki kana

69
Arashi fuku
Mimuro no yama no
momijiba wa
Tatsuta no kawa no
nishiki narikeri

70
Sabishisa ni
yado o tachiidete
nagamureba
izuko mo onaji
aki no yuugure

71
Yū sareba
kadota no inaba
otozurete
ashi no maroya ni
akikaze zo fuku

72
Oto ni kiku
Takashi no hama no
adanami wa
kakeji ya sode no
nure mokoso sure

73
Takasago no
onoe no sakura
sakinikeri
toyama no kasumi
tatazu mo aranan

74
Ukarikeru
hito o Hatsuse no
yamaoroshi

hageshikare to wa
inoranu mono-o

75
Chigiri-okishi
sasemo ga tsuyu o
inochi nite
aware kotoshi no
aki mo inumeri

76
Wata no hara
kogiidete mireba
hisakata no
kumoi ni magau
oki tsu shiranami

77
Se o hayami
iwa ni sekaruru
takigawa no
warete mo sue ni
awan to zo omou

78
Awaji shima
kayou chidori no
naku koe ni
iku yo nezamenu
Suma no sekimori

79
Akikaze ni
tanabiku kumo no
taema yori
more-izuru tsuki no
kage no sayakesa

80
Nagakaran
kokoro mo shirazu
kurokami no
midarete kesa wa
mono o koso omoe

81
Hototogisu
nakitsuru kata o
nagamureba
tada ariake no
tsuki zo nokoreru

82
Omoiwabi
sate mo inochi wa
aru mono-o
uki ni taenu wa
namida nari keri

83
Yo no naka yo
michi koso nakere
omoiiru
yama no oku ni mo
shika zo nakunaru

84
Nagaraeba
mata kono goro ya
shinobaren
ushi to mishi yo zo
ima wa koishiki

85
Yomosugara
monoomou koro wa
akeyarade

neya no hima sae
tsurenakarikeri

86
Nageke tote
tsuki ya wa mono o
omowasuru
kakochigao naru
waga namida kana

87
Murasame no
tsuyu mo mada hinu
maki no ha ni
kiri tachinoboru
aki no yūgure

88
Naniwa-e no
ashi no karine no
hitoyo yue
miotsukushite ya
koiwatarubeki

89
Tama no o yo
taenaba taene
nagaraeba
shinoburu koto no
yowari mo zo suru

90
Misebayana
Ojima no ama no
sode dani mo
nure ni zo nureshi
iro wa kawarazu

91
Kirigirisu
naku ya shimoyo no
samushiro ni
koromo katashiki
hitori ka mo nen

92
Waga sode wa
shiohi ni mienu
oki no ishi no
hito koso shirane
kawaku ma mo nashi

93
Yo no naka wa
tsune ni mogamo na
nagisa kogu
ama no obune no
tsunade kanashi mo

94
Miyoshino no
yama no akikaze
sayo fukete
furusato samuku
koromo utsunari

95
Ōkenaku
uki yo no tami ni
ōu kana
waga tatsu soma ni
sumizome no sode

96
Hana sasou
arashi no niwa no
yuki narade

furiyuku mono wa
waga mi narikeri

97
Konu hito o
Matsuho no ura no
yūnagi ni
yaku ya moshio no
mi mo kogaretsutsu

98
Kaze soyogu
Nara no ogawa no
yūgure wa
misogi zo natsu no
shirushi narikeru

99
Hito mo oshi
hito mo urameshi
ajikinaku
yo o omou yue ni
mono-omou mi wa

100
Momoshiki ya
furuki noki-ba no
shinobu ni mo
nao amari aru
mukashi narikeri

Maps

1. Famous Locations (*Utamakura*) in the *One Hundred Poets*: Heiankyo (Kyoto) and Environs

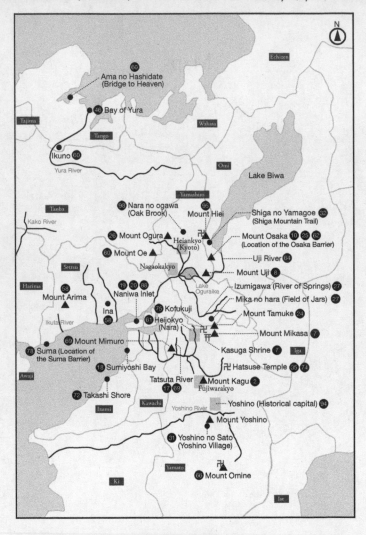

- 🔵 Poem featuring the location
- ● Place
- ▲ Mountain
- — Major river
- ▮ Historical capital
- ▬ Historical province
- 卍 Shrine
- 卍 Temple

2. Famous Locations (*Utamakura*) in the *One Hundred Poets*: Regions Beyond Heiankyo (Kyoto)

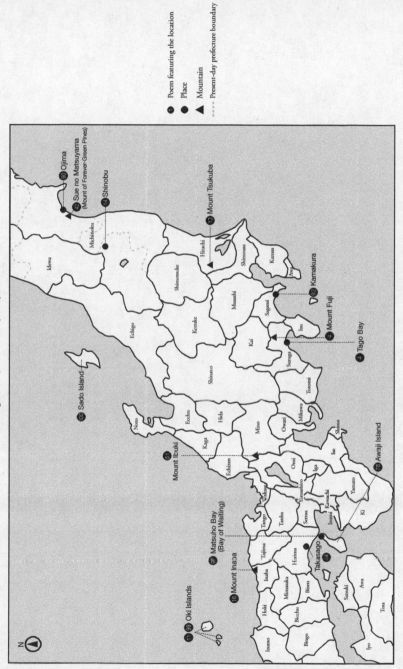

Poem featuring the location
● Place
▲ Mountain
‑‑‑‑ Present-day prefecture boundary

Acknowledgements

For their help with all aspects of the translation, I am indebted to many people. I thank Kaori (Lily) Harada for her help with the translation and the Commentary and my editor, Jessica Harrison, and Kate Parker for her dazzlingly brilliant and meticulous copy-editing. I thank Simon Lewis for introducing me to Penguin and Alexander Smith for his insightful suggestions for translating difficult wordplay. For editorial direction I thank Professor Yasuaki Watanabe and his brilliant student Hikari Okamoto, who helped greatly with the final revisions. I thank Donald Keene for reading the original manuscript and writing the foreword to the first edition. I also thank Janet Lowe and Stephen Payton for their careful reading of the proofs. And I thank Robert Campbell and the faculty of the National Institute of Japanese Literature for their kind support of this book and all my literary translation endeavours.

To my readers, I thank former ambassadors John Neary and Tim Hitchens, my friend of old, Colm Rowan, and Philip Harries, who all brought to their reading of the text outstanding editing skills and a deep knowledge of and sensitivity to poetry. I also thank my staff, Shizuka Sado, Shizuko Goshima, Kosuke Ogasawara and Keita Katayama, for their unfailing support.

Without kind patronage the translation could not have been completed: I thank the Suntory Foundation for their translation grants. Michiko, Maiko and Takao Sato of Kotoku-in, Kamakura, and Norimasa and Rika Nishida are patrons of this and other of my literary translations. Dr Hiroharu Matsuda, his wife and the Matsuda family have supported me for thirty years. And Yayoi Hirayama has provided every kindness. Above all I thank Yuichi Mitsuyama, whose love and pursuit of the truth is an abiding source of inspiration.

I thank my wonderful and inspiring interns Yuka Hattori, Kotaro Hirose, Senju Hanahara, Katsuki Nagakubo and last but not least, Masashi Takeuchi.

I also owe an enormous debt to my beloved friend the late Eileen Kato, who gave many valuable suggestions at every stage of the original translation. No one would be happier than her that this translation of this seminal work is being published by Penguin and disseminated throughout the world.